Scenes of Wonder & Curiosity

Scenes of Wonder & Curiosity

The Photographs & Writings of
Ted Orland

Foreword by Sally Mann

DAVID R. GODINE · PUBLISHER · BOSTON

First published in 1988 by
David R. Godine, Publisher, Inc.
Horticultural Hall
300 Massachusetts Avenue
Boston, Massachusetts 02115

Library of Congress Catalog Card Number 88–45333
ISBN 0–87923–768–8

Library of Congress Cataloging-in-Publication Data

Orland, Ted.
    Scenes of wonder and curiosity.

    1. Orland, Ted—Correspondence.   2. Photography—
Landscapes.   I. Title.
TR140.075A4   1988   770'.92'4 [B]   88–45333
ISBN 0–87923–768–8

First Edition
Printed in the United States of America

SCENES OF WONDER & CURIOSITY

has been set in Palatino, a typeface designed by Hermann Zapf. Named after Giovanbattista Palatino, a Renaissance writing master, it was the first of Zapf's typefaces to be introduced to America. The designs were made in 1948, and the fonts for the complete face were issued between 1950 and 1952.

The book was set in type and printed by Meriden-Stinehour Press at Lunenburg, Vermont, and Meriden, Connecticut. It was bound by Acme Bookbinding Company of Charlestown, Massachusetts. The paper is Mohawk Vellum for the text and Warren LOE Dull for the plates. The book design is by Ted Orland.

FOREWORD

Looking back today, Ted, I almost miss those mutable early years that I now recognize to have been our youth, spent like a found nickel. Your letters bring it all back, of course, and they play for me like a time-lapse movie: events unfold into view, flash by and recede; emotions color the scene, often passionately, and are diluted eventually by the flow of time. A marriage comes and goes; a child grows up and leaves; three more appear, at first tiny specks, swelling into view, then looming large. We move from house to house like jerky little speeded-up cartoon characters; rivers roll, flood, and retreat, anxiety leaks in and smears across, thins out, and is replaced by a wash of serenity. The flow is obscured from time to time, going dark as if for the briefest night, but always reappearing. I am struck by the tenacity of our bond, the resiliency of our imperfect link, as gossamer as a spider's thread, and as durable.

These letters, these photographs, span fifteen years. Viewed from a distance they seem so effortless; there is a perfect rightness about your great art, as if ecstatic creations were all there was. But I know, I remember the quotidian history that fleshes out the picture here. It would seem that there are two different kinds of time, what Hollis Frampton called "historic time"—actual time—and "ecstatic time." Historic time is remarkably unmemorable, consisting of sequential events strung together in speech by the connective phrase, *"and then."* The ticking clock and the passage of years only emphasize the sad truth that life, by and large, is unremarkable, consisting for the most part of a meager sampling of highlights on a dull field. Surely no one but the murderer could know the answer to the question, "Where were you at 4 P.M. on April 21st?"

But when you edit it all down, when you slow the moving picture and zero in upon one freeze-frame of this fast flow, you enter into a different kind of time, that of ecstatic time— not quite accountable, not quite sequential, where the measured passage of linear time is altered or stops altogether.

Frampton tells a marvelous story about a man with the unlikely name of Breedlove, who in a rocket-powered car called *The Spirit of America* broke the world land speed record on the Bonneville Salt Flats. Near the end of his second run, at 620 miles per hour, he lost control of his car and it careened wildly out of control, severing telephone poles, flying through the air, flipping upside down, and crashing into a salt pond.

Incredibly, Breedlove escaped unharmed. Asked by a reporter at the scene to remark on the incident, Breedlove spoke into the microphone for an astonishing hour and thirty-five minutes, during which time he describes in a sequential and deliberate way what occured in a period of 8.7 *seconds.* During the course of the monologue, Breedlove expresses concern that he will bore his listeners and that, with this thought in mind, he is condensing his story for their sake, that he is doing his polite best to make a long story short. According to Frampton, this ecstatic utterance represents a temporal expansion in the ratio of 655 to one.

You and I use the camera to achieve these moments, and in your correspondence—while you express dismay at the dulling daily-ness of your life—you break through into that great joy, that dimension of revelation, and ecstacy, and humor that eludes historic time. The whimsical glint of your keen wit, your clever mind, your gentle heart transcend the mundanity. Your photographs—and your writing—serve as impediments in that fast flow of time, like boulders in a stream that never diminish the force or the volume of the flow, but by virtue of the local turbulence they generate, measure and demonstrate both. Your work is resonant with the vertiginous delight of the stream and the durability of the stone.

Sally Mann
Lexington, Virginia, 1988

Boone Morrison

Ted Orland

Chris Johnson

Robert Langham

Sally Mann

David Bayles

The original Image Continuum Group
1974

INTRODUCTION

IT ALL SEEMS so long ago now. When I first picked up a camera in the mid-1960's, the worthwhile literature of the art consisted of a single work: Edward Weston's *Daybooks*.

Oh, there were others, doubtless, but they remained unpublished or unpublicized, and certainly unknown to me. The same could be said of many photographers, like Diane Arbus or Wynn Bullock, who were producing monumental images for an audience of (with luck) a few friends.

Yet it was, in another sense, a perfectly fine time to plunge into the Art. Everyone was approachable: in those days, being the most famous photographer in the country, plus the proverbial dime, would get you a cup of coffee. Ansel Adams was still trying to sell his *Portfolio IV*; it took years to deplete the edition, perhaps because of its high price—nine dollars a print. Imogen Cunningham's were a whopping ten; Brett Weston, who inherited his father's frugality and taste for artichokes, may be the only sure example of a photographer who actually lived off printsales-as-Art in the 1960's.

Knowing nothing of this, I spotted a tiny space-filler in the back pages of *Modern Photography* early in 1966 noting that Ansel Adams (an artist I'd never met) would be conducting a summer photography workshop in Yosemite Valley (a place I'd never seen). Two weeks for $150. Seemed innocent enough. Changed my life.

Next summer I was back again, this time as Ansel's Workshop Assistant—my primary qualification being that since I only had a 35mm, I could easily enough carry his *real* camera as well. From there it was just a matter of time: I slowly disengaged from my work as a designer, and in 1971 moved to the Monterey Peninsula to work fulltime at Ansel's home.

Working for Ansel brought me into contact with legendary figures like Beaumont Newhall and Imogen Cunningham, while his workshops introduced me to remarkable fellow travellers from my own generation—young photographers like Linda Connor and David Bayles and Sally Mann.

And though I'm a slow learner—my photographs remained straight Adamsonian landscapes for years—this wealth of input inevitably began to yield returns. In early 1973, close friends joined with me in forming a group we titled (rather self-consciously) *The Image Continuum*, and we laid plans for sharing our ideas and in-progress work with other artists via a self-published *Journal*. And prophetically, that same summer at the Yosemite Workshop I met an amazing young photographer-writer named Sally Mann, resulting in a friendship—largely *postal*, since we live at opposite ends of the country—now spanning its fifteenth year.

It is these letters to Sally (along with a sprinkling for the *Journal* and other friends) that comprise the text for this book. Taken together, they encompass a turbulent decade, a time when my own vision was evolving and maturing rapidly, a time when fine art photography finally began reaching an audience beyond one's fellow photographers.

I've tried to remain true to the spirit of those times while paring everything down to book length. I realize that some names appearing in the text will be unfamiliar to you at first, but you'll pick them up from context soon enough (and if you're really curious you can always peek at the biographical notes in the Afterword). Also, you should know there are a few people very special to me—like my son Jon and my partner Frances—who rarely appear in these pages at all.

All that's just to say that while this book is autobiographical, it is definitely not an autobiography—rather, it's more about the *process* of being an artist, about the way time and circumstance, event and emotion surround the moment the shutter is opened. I'd like to think of my experiences as providing an affirmation to younger artists that the path they have chosen *does* lead somewhere, that there are fellow travellers on that path, and that those who are now a few steps further down the path are really no different—perhaps only a bit older.

Ted Orland
Santa Cruz, 1988

Ansel Adams and Imogen Cunningham
Awarding Jerry Uelsmann
the Title of
Honorary West Coast Photographer
at Weston Beach, Pt. Lobos, 1969

LETTERS

July 1973

MINOR WHITE has been staying here at Ansel's this week while teaching a Friends of Photography Workshop. I still haven't gotten up the courage to talk with him, but I love the excitement he brings as he comes running back from the beach each noontime, barefoot and unshaven and laughing, bearing handfuls of rollfilm to develop, and leaving Ansel's darkroom festooned with more new negatives than it's seen in years. Better yet, he's even gracious and charming, sporting an often hilarious irreverence toward the "fuzzy-minded mysticism" (his term) that has given him such guru-like status amongst the faithful.

> Q: *What are followers of Minor White called?*
> A: *minor whites.*

Then this afternoon Brett Weston dropped by (accompanied as always by his larger-than-lifesize ego) to join Minor & AA for drinks, and the resulting conversational counterpoint would have impressed J. S. Bach himself! Brett loves to express disdain for AA's overtly scientific approach to art, and after a couple of shots of whiskey he said, "You know, Ansel, dear friend, Dad's whole house and studio cost less to build than your darkroom *sink*" (True). But soon enough Ansel's Swiftian wit neutralized Brett's barb as he agreeably donned the Mantle of Scientism and intoned with Great Solemnity:

> *Said Einstein, I have an Equation*
> *Which Newton might find Rabelaisian.*
> *Let V be Virginity, approaching Infinity,*
> *And U be a constant persuasion.*
> *Now if V be inverted*
> *And U be inserted,*
> *The Proof is a Relative, he asserted.*

Minor, for his part, talked of opening his workshop session this evening by having everyone sit in a circle and hold hands and chant "OMMMMM . . . " Now that doesn't seem overly radical, not for *California*, but when I asked Ansel later whether he planned to attend, he paused, picking his words very carefully, and said, "Minor is one of my closest friends; I've known him for many years; he's a great photographer; he's an inspiring teacher; I'm sure his session will be very enlightening . . . *but I refuse to meditate!!*"

August 1973

THE ECONOMY, I fear, has stunted my artistic growth: I can't afford an air conditioner, and sharing my 4 x 7 foot darkroom with the water heater in August is a losing proposition—I have to work naked, and feed an ice-cube to the developer tray with each print. Perhaps I'll stick to photographing in the summer, and printing in the winter. After all, I wouldn't be the first artist to be influenced by logic: when I asked Barbara Crane how she came to do the nude studies of her daughters, she replied, "In Chicago you simply don't photograph outdoors in the winter, and the girls were the only props I had around the house."

Or, as Weston said, "By the way, Brett, on the way home would you pick up a pepper? . . ."

January 1974

YESTERDAY ANSEL threw his Annual New Year's Day Bash, to which he habitually invites *everyone*—the Postman, Brett Weston, the Japanese cleaning lady, Wynn Bullock, just everyone. Chris Johnson and Marty came down for the occasion and stayed at our house, giving us time before the party to talk seriously about the Image Continuum, and hours afterward to joust in more animated—but doubtless less coherent—fashion about the general state of the Art. In the course of things Chris advanced this wonderfully Zen-like hypothesis which he says will serve as the core for his *Image Continuum Journal* article:

You can only photograph what you see;
You can only see what you feel;
You can only feel what you are
—thus you can only photograph what you are.

It's twilight again now; Ansel and I have been standing at the window hunting for comets and whales, sighting many of the latter but as yet none of the former. Still, with the whales spouting and arching their tails amid great swells rolling in from distant off-shore storms, and the sun giving off a brilliant green flash at the instant of setting—it all leaves me wondering by what privilege I should be witness to it all.

February 1974

I MEANDERED SOUTHWARD to Los Angeles Friday, mostly following the abandoned frontage roads that parallel the freeway. It's my favorite mode of travel: loping along at 40 mph, windows down and music up, watching for funky buildings and abandoned treasures. Along the way I was rewarded with a vista of oil wells sprouting indiscriminately among cabbage patches, and another where Man's Destiny To Control the Environment took the unlikely form of a river under construction. I even convinced a giant spherical water tower to pose for a 20th-century *Moonrise.*

See *Exhibit A,* Fotograf.

But very best among my finds was the All-American metropolis: FAT CITY, replete with an Official Sign proclaiming its population of 30,000, uh, *cattle.*

Imagine a square mile of stockyard laid out in the form of tidy residential streets complete with light poles and street signs at the corners, and curbs fashioned into troughs stuffed with feed poured from huge trucks that slowly circle the neighborhood. But OHOHOHO the true Orwellian touch hit home when I stepped out of the bus to make a picture and discovered that those poles contain not only street lights (to keep the residents awake and eating 24 hours a day), but also *loudspeakers* to keep them content by playing the local radio station at top volume!

Exhibit A

Yessirree, true middle-class cow suburbia, its residents lulled into sedentary obesity with a steady supply of country western music (and Safeway ads for this week's steak special) . . .

The rationale for this odyssey was a regional meeting of the Society for Photographic Education (S.P.E.), which I just joined and then perversely kept confusing with Photographic Society of America (P.S.A.), which it decidedly is *not.* But anyway, it did give me the chance to meet some well-known photographers like Arthur Taussig, Robert Heinecken, and Darryl Curran, whom I had only known from halftones on the printed page.

It also gave me a sobering view of the state of the photo-education biz—the mood became pretty grim once the topic turned to life in the classroom! The general consensus seemed to be that teaching leaves one totally drained of creative energy for personal work after giving heart and soul to students all day. But personally, I'd be tempted to test that consensus; I've been working 8–12 hours a day for other people for eleven years now, and the idea of teaching, with all those wonderful blocks of free time over summer and holidays . . . well, it sure sounds good to me!

May 1974

OFF AT 6 AM today, bound for the Bancroft Library's Rare Book Room in search for memorabilia of early Yo-Semite. But I think it was the trip itself I savored most, heading north along foggy Highway 1, pausing to scan the Pacific rim a dozen times as viewfinder dictated. It was all just too pretty to take seriously, but I finally succumbed anyway and made a 4 x 5 that has Brett Weston written all over it. You know, I could make Big Bucks in this biz if photographers returned to the 19th century practice of selling *negatives* to each other—I've got a closetful of embarrassingly fine-grained Weston look-alikes that someone like Fred Picker would just die for.

Later the fog melted into summer heat as I crossed the Bay Bridge and neared the UC Berkeley campus. Walking in the last few blocks along Telegraph Avenue, the ambience changed from Weston to Arbus faster than you could say "reciprocity failure"! You wonder where all the Flower Children who blossomed in Haight-Asbury have gone? I'll tell you: they've gone to seed in Berkeley—crowds of benignly drugged and bronzed bodies, the male variants stript to the waist and the female nearly so, all engaged in the peculiarly Californian occupation of simply *being visible.*

Telegraph Ave was strewn with sidewalk capitalists—I bought handmade sandals for myself, and feather earrings for Linda—interspersed with rolling foodstands trundling aromatic Arabic and Mexican and Natural Organic Twinkies. Entering campus via Sather Gate, I first ran a gauntlet of Hari Krishnas (Krishni?) sitting beneath giant sunshades chanting and playing bells and drums and indescribable East Indian instruments, and then passed their secular equivalent hawking Red Brigade literature and playing guitars (with instrument cases opened hopefully at their feet for Offerings).

Rounding another corner, I heard more chanting—well, *shouting*—which quickly materialized into several hundred rampaging students engaged in taking over one of the buildings; I learned later they were occupying the *Criminology* Building, to prevent the Administration from balancing its budget by closing that Department . . . all of which left the local militia in a quandary, since for once they found themselves rooting for the students. (*Ergo*, they spared the tear-gas today).

But finally I reached my destination, plunked down into one of the Library's soft leather chairs, and looked across the table to a kindly gentleman who was a thousand miles and several hundred years off in another world, lovingly perusing an original edition of the Kelmscott *Chaucer*. Scenes of Wonder and Curiosity in California.

Summer 1974

POPULAR ARTISTE zat I am, I spent ze day filling print orders . . . well, *trades* actually, money apparently not yet being a recognized medium of exchange for my work. Fortunately for the Production Department, however, that oval-shaped pic of the flying person over San Francisco Bay is emerging as the three-penny opera equivalent to *Moonrise, Hernandez*—I've had six requests for same this month alone! So I took the plunge into decadent giantism by cutting an oval printing template that yields 11 x 14's (my first!), and cranked out a bunch—in trade for which I should eventually receive a Roger Minick print, a Mark Citret print, a Sally Mann print, and a copy of *Edward Weston, Fifty Years*. Not bad for an afternoon, viewed that way. (And you know, I don't even remember making the picture—it was one of a hundred hand-held grab-shots I made that day.)

Now today, that's another matter entirely: Whish, squeak, clunk; wait three minutes; un-clunk, squeak, un-swish print from the drymount press. Yes, Man the Hunter has evolved to an era of Division of Labor, working out at that hard leading edge of industrial technology, applying his skill and intellect to controlling the delicate and intricate machinery that makes it possible for . . . for . . . tourists to buy expensive souvenirs. I'm told the true test of your fitness for a profession turns upon your ability to enjoy the *drudgery* it involves, and four hours at the drymount press is enough to leave that issue still more than a bit in doubt for me. Perhaps it's just that counting all those seconds serves as an occasionally morbid reminder that the real cause of death is *birth.*

August 1974

THE LAST DAY of the month is at hand, bringing *freedom* at its close! Cheers!!—after eleven years of non-stop fulltime jobs, I'm finally charting a fundamental change in course. Looking back, I sometimes think the only times of real changes in my life have come either from making a wildly non-rational choice to abandon the predictable, or from disaster being thrust upon me from the outside—and you could probably find ample evidence of both forces at work here. But though my fantasies run amok at the prospects for my forthcoming life of leisure, I also plan to continue part-time with Ansel, printing his Special Edition Yosemite pics. Not that I'm likely to get rich doing it: I get paid on a piecework basis . . . a whopping one dollar per print!

November 1974

I GUESS MOST OF US inhabit equivalent, if separate, worlds. I share my world with a spouse-person & child, a precarious bank account, a Wanderlust that sets in when I have no new negatives to print, and a few special friends I visit so rarely my existence is probably mere folk legend amongst them.

And I face this paradox: that in my mind Necessity and Fantasy and Reality keep crossing—that what is Necessity in the short run is irrelevant in the long run, that what is Fantasy in the short run proves fundamental in the long run . . . and that Reality is largely a world of my own devising. I do always feel a certain envy for others in our [Image Continuum] Group, but doubt I would actually enjoy trading places with any of you for long, any more than I really enjoy backpacking despite my envy for the life John Muir led.

I used to think I was in control of what I photographed; but in truth the meaning of my images becomes apparent only later, while their level of intensity reverberates in Real Time—even before the exposure—like traces upon a seismograph. You know how it is, that sudden spine-tingling sensation (after hours of mindless wandering) when a fleeting concordance of time & space startles your mind, saying, "Look, *there!*"

Ansel likes to say that Nature offers only shapes, upon which the discipline of our mind imposes form. But if the conscious mind is adept at explaining and manipulating the patterns of nature, it sure is a clumsy tool for initially sensing and responding to them in the first place. We enjoy delegating instinct and intuition to other species—accepting it as quite natural, say, that migratory birds navigate at night by tracking the stars, and on *cloudy* nights by responding to the Earth's astonishingly weak north magnetic field(!). But we really want to believe that our own actions are a matter of Free Will, that we are above influence by any directions less intellectually invasive than a flashing "Don't Walk" sign.

The pessimist in me, however, suspects that a great majority of people operate from a position of neither intuition *nor* consciousness. I rather tend to Oespensky's view that most people spend their days in a state of sleep, guided along paths laid out by habit or by others. The need is to awaken from that state, recognize the surrounding chaos, and give yourself permission to create from it your own cosmology. Viewed from that perspective, my images *do* define my existence, by bringing to consciousness and form my intuitive response to the world.

And another thing: I used to think that developing as an artist consisted largely of things like keeping an open and probing mind, analyzing the significant elements in the landscape, reading/discussing/attending the Arts, and so on. Lately I've adopted a much simpler view: that all one really needs is *Time*—time to do one hell of a lot of work! And time is created not by philosophizing about it, but by the discouragingly tangible bit-by-bit pushing aside of inessential tasks and distractions.

It's a delicate task—matching input with output, life with art. Yet the need is exactly that: to integrate *all* the threads of one's existence until they become a working part of the total fabric. Thoreau says at some point in *Walden*, ". . . if one advances confidently in the direction of his dreams, and endeavors to live the life he has imagined, he will meet with a success unexpected in common hours." To accomplish *anything* is to do no more than that.

A terminal landscape

December 1974

AT SUNSET today I happened upon this truly archetypal scene, one that offered up in one composition *all* the elements that have been floating separately through my images the past couple of years! In the foreground stood ten-foot tall stalks of wild pampas grass, windblown, trampled by deer, stretching into the distance until their advance was interrupted by a flock of domesticated mobile homes, then resuming (but now interspersed with tidbits of civilization) into the distance, finally terminating on the horizon with the faint silhouette of a great factory.

At first I was ecstatic, clambering onto my VW roof with tripod & camera & the usual tons of baggage. Then, while catching my breath, it suddenly dawned on me that a lot of that baggage was *mental*—that making this picture was just *too easy*. Oh, I went ahead and made a record shot anyway, but it was like picking overripe fruit—the time for such Terminal Landscapes has passed now that I've grown accustomed to their strangeness . . . I need to move on to ideas that still hover at the edge of my consciousness.

November 1974

I SPENT THIS AFTERNOON with Wynn Bullock, sitting in his skylit studio/library, surrounded by writings of Einstein & Russell & Whitehead. Ostensibly we were planning his upcoming UC Extension Workshop, but digressed almost instantly into discussing the much richer cosmology Wynn explores through his images.

It was for the most part Wynn's monologue—I tried a *dia*logue the first time we met, and backed off after five minutes with the distinct sensation that he had burnt out half the synapses in my brain from sensory overload. But for me, trapped out here in f/64 territory where words themselves are suspect, it's a breath of fresh air to find someone who positively thrives upon discussing his art; better yet, he often expresses his ideas in the form of (self-directed) questions, inviting responses and challenges. How heartening to find Wynn, at this stage of his life, still searching and probing and producing new work, rather than codifying and inscribing old work as Commandments on great stone tablets!

The painful corollary to that, alas, is having to listen to the asshole who is trying to worm himself into the role of Wynn's "financial adviser." Said asshole strutted in to complain to me today that Wynn and Dave Bohn had some cockeyed idea about making a "fine" Announcement (i.e. typeset, printed on fine paper) for Wynn's forthcoming Portfolio; so this guy says he'll convince Wynn there's no *need* for doing it well, since Wynn is famous enough that he could—and therefore *should*—save money by just sending out mimeographed order blanks. Well how do you come to grips with a mentality like that, especially when he "proves" his point by the example that his stockbroker is buying one because it's a "good investment," and his lawyer is buying one because "he can donate it somewhere for a tax write-off"?

As that conversation unfolded, I kept thinking back to Wynn himself, one of the gentle and good visual philosophers of this world. At age seventy he has been staring Death in the face for the past year after three cancer operations, and has chosen now to offer a small summation from his life's work in Portfolio form. I think of Wynn, and then I watch the vultures circling around, eyeing his approaching death as an economic feast, looking for the easiest way to squeeze a profit for themselves from his life, and arrogantly dismissing the whole idea of Quality as one of those inscrutable concepts that only an artist would be foolish enough to value. . . .

January 1975

REMEMBER THIS as the day California Struck Back with weather only an Easterner would believe! So we bade farewell to David [Bayles] and he drove off into the crimson sunrise gloomily recounting how there was no snow in the Valley of the Yosemite, no snow in the surrounding High Sierra, and as a matter of fact no interesting weather anywhere in this whole dumb state—and so he drove off and is now stranded for the night in Watsonville, not twenty-five miles from here, because the *Coastal* range is impassable with snowdrifts. *Red sun at morn, sailor be warned.*

But oh such a good week with David here, filled to all the corners, and even the three days of drudgery at the drymount press was worth it for the conversation.

There was one particular day, perhaps it was last Wednesday, ostensibly spent mounting prints into [*Image Continuum*] *Journal II*, but memorable really for its conversation—an amazing 10 or 12 hours probing the central question of How, and Why, David & I make photographs. We locked horns all the way, though any potential for real anger was periodically disarmed by our chronic weakness for taking (benign) Cheap Shots—*e.g.* David bowing gracefully to my greater experience in graphic design with the statement, "You could write everything I know about graphic design on the head of a pin . . . and everything I *care* about it on the *point!*"

Even now it all seems too complex, perhaps too subtle as well, to whack down into a few sentences on the electric typewriter, but I think I'll try anyway since the understanding gained from that interchange is far greater than the usual mushy, knowledge-like substitute that remains after thoughts not fully resolved are simply *agreed upon* in order to be done

with them. This was one line of thought that was carried through to the end and nailed to the wall—carried past the point of dropping the subject to avoid becoming argumentative, past the point of agreeing we were only quibbling over semantics in order to mask our real differences.

The jumping-off point was this: that almost everyone who wrote anything for *Journal II*, including you & me, wrote about the value of intuition in the creative process. Everyone but David, who proceeded to write about how intuition was just so much Bullshit. Well my initial reaction was that he was donning his familiar iconoclast's hat. But Not So!—and therein began our attempt to unravel exactly *how*, comparatively speaking, David & I work. Amongst much fun-making over my attempts to describe the spine-tingling feeling of rightness that a scene sometimes provokes in me, it became clear that David actually does not experience that at all, ever.

We compared a typical outing: A) Me, typically, wandering along with camera until some scene grabs me, and God points down from the sky shouting "f/8 at a 6oth!"; B) David, typically, (in his words as best I can) driving along and seeing a forest beside the road, and knowing from experience that the light would be good in there, and from the terrain that ferns would be growing in there, and figuring that he can stop and get out and wander through the woods and pretty soon will find some ferns that he "*can work up into a photograph.*" No intuitive flashes, no "inspiration"—just hard work.

But, I asked, if there is no triggering mechanism, then why *there*, why *ferns*?—after all there are zillions of potential photographs being passed every moment that are *not* being taken. The answer, as it unfolded, came down to a more universal breakpoint: I am at heart a Romantic; David, by comparison, is a Classicist. For me, a fern (as subject) is not a fern, but an Equivalent I respond to emotionally, and scrutinize with my intellect only much later. For David a fern is equally not a fern, but rather (he might say) an opportune subject for working out a theory he has about the organization of random objects on a flat field. It's as simple, or complex, as organizing the world in the left-hemisphere of your brain, or the right. . . .

January 1975

P A U L C A P O N I G R O appeared unexpectedly at our door-step last weekend, having inexplicably chosen to return to Santa Fe from Los Angeles *via* Carmel. Linda & I happily gave him our car to explore the coast for an afternoon, accepted his treat to an elegant sushi dinner at the local Japanese restaurant, put him up for the night—and drove him off to the airport to catch the Red-eye Special out the next morning.

I can't say just why he made that strange one-day loop out to see us, but I guess what remains in my mind most strongly is our conversation from dinner. Paul & I have equivalent family structures—a wife & a 9-year-old son—and he talked about the problems he has finding the free time and peace of mind he needs to work creatively, about the need to just get away from family and talk with other people occasionally . . . and of how actions like that are so often viewed as a threat or a rejection by Eleanor.

For me, hearing those words was an experience akin to *deja vu*—hearing him express all my concerns, all my problems here . . . as *his*. Clearly the storm clouds swirl around both our lives these days, and perhaps I find it comforting (in some perverse way) to know that even my personal gods also live in the real world. . . .

Winter 1975

M Y T I N Y R O O M is cluttered today with the reminders of already-missed deadlines, but that seems fair trade for a weekend filled with memories of roaming two hundred miles a day with car and camera . . . memories of light and spaces so exciting I searched for images sixteen hours a day, skipping meals until darkness finally fell.

Soon there will be proofsheets, but for now a couple of 4 x 5 Polaroids will have to suffice. I sure love my Toyo View groundglass, its tidily inscribed gridlines fairly pandering to my Freudian desire to compose scenes into T O T A L S Y M-M E T R Y. The freeway pic I had tried twice before without success, and this last version is about as good (or symmetrical)

as it's going to get, with the freeway pylon & pole vertically dead-center, and the horizon line equally so horizontally. So much for intuition, eh?

Now the other picture . . . well, after what I went through to get it, you damn well better like it! Looks innocuous enough, I admit: a torn netting supported by a single pole—*centered*, of course—stretched across a forest backdrop, with atmosphere and architecture filling in space.

Unfortunately, that shredded safety netting, which obviously wasn't functional, enclosed a golf driving range, which obviously *was*. So for ten minutes I stood next to the "275 Y A R D S" marker, trying to maintain a contemplative Zen-like serenity appropriate to an Artiste, while every ten seconds or so there would be a *!THUNK!* and a golf ball at my feet, or ten feet in front of me, or ten feet *beyond* me. Let's see: if I place the sky on Zone . . . *sssssssssTHUNK!* . . . VIII and the forest on Zone III and add a yellow . . . *sssssssssssssssssssssss THUNK!!* . . . filter, then it should be 1/30th at . . . *ssssssssssssss*—f/22—*ssssss*. . . .

Golf range

THE YOSEMITE VALLEY
Summer 1973

18

FOREST, SAN FRANCISCO
1975

(opposite)
THE ENTROPY CELEBRATION
A Positive Attitude Toward the Energy Crisis
1973

ENTRANCE TO BIKE TRAIL
1974

KULTURE ADVANCING ACROSS CALIFORNIA
1980

GATE & GUARD DOG
1975

DEAD TYRANNOSAURUS
1976

WINTER SWIMMING
1976

ANGELS DOING IT!
(Where Did You Think Cherubs Came From?)
1978

LOTS OF LITTLE DEAD DOGGIES ON THEIR WAY TO DOGGIE HEAVEN
1976

EVEN ANSEL ADAMS HAS TO EARN A LIVING
1973

February 1975

I WAS PRINTING a lifetime supply of *Moons & Half Domes* at Ansel's today when I sensed a commotion outside. So I opened the darkroom door and there—*blink*—stood Imogen Cunningham! Well I was still half-blinded by the light—but she wasn't.

"Good Heavens!" she exclaimed, "I thought you were dead—you haven't come to visit me since you photographed me in my Eames chair three years ago!" (True.)

Then she added, "Oh yes, I saw your print in that *Journal* thing Chris Johnson gave me. But you know what's wrong with that? It's too precious! You should be out having exhibits and showing your work to the whole world instead of putting it into pretty little boxes—that's too much work!"

Well, it turned out she was here on assignment from *People Magazine*(!) to photograph Ansel. Of course he immediately set about returning the favor, and together they were a *trip*—Ansel armed with his electric Hasselblad, and Imogen sporting an ancient twin-lens Rollei.

Her working method was simplicity itself: she would squint at her vintage Weston meter, say "f/8 looks right—what do you think?" and without pausing for an answer fire off a flurry of hand-held shots. It was *Shoot-out at OK Corral* and Imogen won hands down. By the time Ansel unholstered the right camera body (electric), lens (100mm), finder (prism), film (Plus-X), film-back (N+ dev.), lightmeter (Pentax spot) and tripod (Bogen), Imogen had already fired off three dozen shots. "Every one of them perfect," she modestly allowed.

Imogen does seem to delight in tweaking Ansel's ego—enough so that I've heard AA comment wryly that she has *acetic acid* in her veins—and she zinged him with another at lunch. Virginia [Adams] had outdone herself preparing a wonderful feast (all the more appealing to me since my budget hasn't allowed for lunches since the beginning of the year); better yet, our ranks had grown with the unexpected arrival of pianist Cristov Eschenbach, who was in Monterey to give a private recital. So Ansel, surrounded by friends and family and fine food, was in a buoyantly expansive mood, and pretty soon commandeered everyone's attention with an animated

description of his darkroom techniques. Well, Imogen remained uncharacteristically silent for a long time as Ansel expounded on filmbase fog and double hypo baths and selenium toner and the like, but the moment he hit the word "Dektol" she stopped him cold in mid-sentence.

"*Dektol!*" she said. "Oh yes, I remember when that formula first came out. That was in *six*. Then, about nineteen-*twelve*, they began selling it pre-packaged . . ."

Well, I'll tell you, it slowed down the conversation *real fast* to realize we were talking with someone who's been photographing for more than half the time that's passed since the medium was *invented* . . .

Imogen

April 1975

UNEMPLOYMENT HAS its compensations, allowing you time to write your friends, go for a walk when Spirit moves you (she usually moves me with a nudge of her cold nose) and do your part for ecology by acting as a passive solar collector. You also learn not to spend money. I'm living off boxes of photo paper bought in an earlier era of affluence, off little bottles of hypo siphoned from Ansel's twenty-five gallon steel tanks. Like Rommel's *Afrika Korps* advancing on captured gasoline stocks, it works only as long as you KEEP GOING—one step back and it becomes a rout! Soon I'll *have* to sell a print or two for funds to move ahead.

But at least it's my own work filling my life nowadays; I've finished the first prints from new negatives I took this spring, and viewing the results today, all dry and spotted, I'm delighted! Better, I think, to spend the next month preparing for a Show of my own photographs than for one of Ansel's.

I must admit, though, that printing day itself is another matter entirely: my emotional center slides progressively into despair as my favorite new negative turns out to be scratched or blurred, the chemicals perversely refuse to stay anywhere near 68 degrees, the voltage fluctuates erratically, and the drying prints look too light or dark or contrasty or flat or ill-composed, or just plain *stupid*! I am not your Favorite Person at 10 PM of Darkroom Day!

Spring 1975

ARTISTS AND IDIOTS, according to Ben Maddow, share in common the tendency to continue functioning just like they always do, regardless of all hell breaking loose around them. Perhaps so, but when tensions swirl around me too closely, I sure do long for a cabin retreat like yours. There's something reassuring about the *scale* of the Virginia landscape, about the way it lets you walk in and be swallowed up by its moist leafiness. Out here in California you can only stand back twelve miles and look—it's beautiful, but dry and austere.

And another thing: in the East, if you ignore a cleared vacant lot for a dozen years, you'll return to find *woods*. Here, that patch would remain barren forever, but for the slow accretion of dead mattresses, rusting car skeletons, spray-painted graffiti, and enough broken glass to open your own recycling center. Recent disinterest notwithstanding, I think I really could make a go of photographing straight landscapes in your countryside, where Nature is as enveloping and all-pervasive as Freeways are here.

Summer 1975

NOT EVERYONE maintains quite the reverence for history I do. I was over at Brett's yesterday for a couple of hours of beer & talk, mostly just for the pleasure of listening to his reminiscences about people he has known seemingly forever.

Like Imogen: he's known her for FIFTY-TWO years, since he was eight years old. "And she was just as homely then as she is now!" he graciously notes.

Or Frederick Sommer: "He and Dad were great friends. When Dad died I inherited a big pile of Sommer's prints"—indicating about a 3-inch stack with his fingers—"And you know what I did with them, Ted Boy? *I tossed them out*—sickest crap I ever saw in my life!"

But you know, I really do love Brett—there's a wonderful genuineness underlying even his wildest posturing. Like Sommer or Chappell or Bohn or Atget, he's one of Peck's Bad Boys of Photography: he ignored the critics, went his own direction, did exactly what he wanted—and did it so well the art world was eventually forced to circle back to admit him on his own terms.

For myself, perhaps I'd do best to stick just to reminiscences, period, considering the disasters attendant to my last outing with a camera. It was my first pass at nude photography, and with cool professional unruffled aplomb I proceeded to: A) shoot a dozen spectacular pictures . . . all on the same sheet of film; and B) take another dozen totally blank frames by cleverly setting the mirror lock-up button on my Mamiya such that I was really only flipping up the mirror each time I "took a picture." T. Orland, Professional Photographer!

Well, I'm not the only one to run into problems.
I sent Morley Baer the same model to work with,
and he couldn't get the knack of it either.

June 1975

ANOTHER YOSEMITE SUMMER WORKSHOP come and gone, fleetingly memorable as The Year The White House Came To Visit (in the form of Susan Ford). Susan is your typical struggling young photographer . . . allowing for the fact that *Holiday Magazine* has offered her three hundred dollars per print—sight unseen—for *anything* she cares to submit. But it's all OK—she's bright enough to survive this fleeting bout with media-created fame. And actually, being seventeen and attractive and athletic, she fit right in with everyone else as we scrambled over the rocks. It *was* a bit strange, though, to have all those unsmiling men in oddly lumpy business suits with walkie-talkies constantly trailing over the granite slopes behind her.

But the best fun came when she spent an evening regaling a bunch of us at my cabin with lurid White House tales. LIKE: did you know that during Johnson's term they had to plant tall shrubbery around the White House because Lyndon preferred peeing out the window to using the bathroom? (That story alone saved me the price of a subscription to *National Enquirer.*) Or that Tricia & Eddie Cox always slept in separate bedrooms. (Do I look surprised?) Or that both LBJ & Nixon were alcoholics—the latter example punctuated by Susan's animated description (quoting a W.H. maid) of Nixon, totally smashed, *crawling* out of the W.H. elevator and across the Oval Office rug to pull himself up onto the piano to play *America The Beautiful*!

Paparazzi and frivolity notwithstanding, this Workshop had the unsettling feature of being the first at which I did not even attempt any "real" photographs. I feel momentarily lost . . . I have no interest anymore in the easy mark offered by straight landscapes, but I'm as yet unsure how to apply my new-found interest in portraiture. In fact I wish I could even understand just what constitutes portraiture. I always think of my pictures of friends as personal mnemonics for memories that would be meaningless to others; or, if my friends are famous, I imagine their fame rather than my vision makes the image attractive to others.

The real problem, I think, is deciding where to strike the balance between the universal and the particular—between a world like August Sander's that captures a whole society in one face, and a world like Julia Margaret Cameron's that searches for the uniqueness of each personality. Maybe I'll save these doubts for the next issue of the *Journal*— I seem to have run through all the answers I have, and now only the questions remain.

August 1975

THE FRIENDS OF PHOTOGRAPHY staged a potluck dinner for their Members' Workshop Saturday night, corralling me into service for the evening session that followed. This consisted of herding several instructor-types into the center of a theatre-in-the-round, appointing Al Weber as Moderator (can you picture Al as a moderating influence?) and fearlessly plunging into what was heralded as a search for the definition and direction (and by inference the proper defense) of "West Coast Photography."

Well, as luck would have it, another of the instructors that evening was one of our local Orthodox Carmelites who uses an 8x10 viewcamera, f/64, trees, rocks, water, pyro and amidol in every photograph. So Ol' Ted, he just lay low, half-listening to the cacophony of non sequiturs applied in rebuttal to logical fallacies, and thinking Al had the right idea to get smashed before it all began, when the aforementioned True Believer rose to Defend The Faith.

And Verily He Sayeth These Things: that he was TIRED of West Coast Photography being dumped on, that there is nothing wrong with photographing beauty and we should be PROUD to follow the WestCoastTradition and anyway it's a lot healthier than photographing trash cans, but that there seemed to be some people who didn't share that view and in fact there was one person who has even written articles published in a Journal—*Hmmm, you don't suppose*—saying that he saw a Show at the Monterey Art Museum where all the work was dull WestCoastPhotography except for the one set that had *people* in it—*uh oh!*—and if he feels WestCoastPhotography is dead because it's serious and has no people in it he should get up and defend that view and that person is here in the room and his name is TED ORLAND!

Blink! Who, me? Well luckily I had drifted back from Fantasyland just in time to realize he was quoting from letters of mine we published in *Journal 1*! And actually I was delighted, if only to learn that the *Journal* has sent shock waves to such aesthetically distant shores! I was also fairly mellow by that point in the evening, and refrained from launching into my Anti-Christ lecture on the Nine Zones of Hell reserved specifically for photographs of peeling paint, backlit windows, ghost town buildings, sand dunes, black skies, etc.

Instead, I just noted mildly that West Coast Tradition encourages photographers to limit themselves to subject matter they can safely encompass with their technique, and encourages viewers to ignore content and concentrate upon the virtuoso rendering of tones. In essence, it discourages risk-taking by either maker or viewer—and that's not healthy. It's like, in Olympic diving competition they don't give you high points for doing even the *perfect* swan dive off the low board—without challenge there is a limit to perfection that will quickly be reached by many . . .

August 1975

CAPONIGRO ARRIVED on the Peninsula last week, having decided in his typically inscrutable fashion that *this*—well, Ansel's darkroom, to be exact—was where he needed to be to make the repro prints for his forthcoming *Landscape* book. But after a day or two, I got this furtive call—I picture him standing at a pay phone, wearing a trench coat with upturned collar—asking, "I was wondering if you knew anyone else around here who has a 5 x 7 enlarger?" (Something tells me he already knew.) "*Really?* Maybe you can help me out. Ansel and Virginia are being too good to me—every meal is like an Official State Dinner—but I'm not getting any work done! Do you suppose I could come hide out *incognito* at your place for a few days to make these prints?"

So I've left home each morning, returning each evening to find twenty or more new Caponigro prints washing in my darkroom or drying on bath towels on the living room floor. (Not a bad find, eh? Did I ever tell you about the time I was sorting through old cartons at Ansel's and uncovered eighteen mint Edward Weston photographs? I instantly ran to show Ansel these *valuable* prints I'd found . . . realizing only later that I'd had to plough through several FEET of Ansel Adam's prints to reach them.)

But I digress—I wanted to talk about the evenings, maybe about last evening. It unfolded slowly, beginning with a fruitless search for friends with a piano that Paul could practice on, but settling for coffee and conversation at one of Carmel's three-quarter-scale gingerbread-architecture cafes.

I've tried to reconstruct those conversations, but words alone seem barren, deprived of the silences and gestures and the smell of pipe smoke and cinnamon coffee. (Paul & I would probably drive most people crazy, the both of us considering a ten minute reflective pause in the middle of a conversation entirely natural.) Other revelations come from seeing his pictures "unedited" and listening to him talk his way through the dozen variants he made to reach the final print—never describing them in terms like "too dark" or "too contrasty," but always by whether they captured the *feeling* of some part of the scene that he knew was there, and had only to coax from the negative. I'm reminded of the story about Michaelangelo, who when asked how he carved such perfect figures, responded—quite truthfully I'm sure—that the figure *was already there* inside the stone, and that his job was simply to chip away the marble that *wasn't* part of the Madonna.

Paul, I think, has that same ability to see the world with absolute clarity, using his camera to crop out the inessential parts and thereby reveal his understanding. The way he put it was, "You have to keep your eye on the light at the end of the tunnel, and ignore everything else. That everything else— the affairs, the lack of black in the prints, the jobs—are just tests, just distractions. There *is* chaos out there, but whether you remain at the mercy of the chaos depends on whether you see anything beyond the chaos." For myself, I fear it's all I can do to make my *memories* coherent—glimpses of the future are rare indeed.

THE IMAGE CONTINUUM
JOURNAL 2

JANUARY 1975

Contributors to this issue:

Ansel Adams	Jim Hill	Sally Mann	Mark Power
Frances Baer	Wendy Hill	Robert Minden	David Pond-Smith
Morley Baer	Chris Johnson	Roger Minick	Rosamond Purcell
David Bayles	Robert Langham	Boone Morrison	Nancy Simmerman
Dave Bohn	Norman Locks	Morgan Mussell	Steve Szabo
Wynn Bullock	Mary Ann Lynch	Ted Orland	Ronald Wohlauer

Original Prints in the Portfolio section:

ANSEL ADAMS My Parents, Virginia Best, & Aunt Millie, at the old Family Residence on 17th St., San Francisco, ca.1927. (Printed from the original glass plate by Ted Orland)

MORLEY BAER Cortijo de la Maravilla, Spain, 1958.

DAVID BAYLES Untitled, 1975.

DAVE BOHN In The Valley of Ten Thousand Smokes; Katmai National Monument, Alaska, August 1973.

WYNN BULLOCK Photogram, ca.1940.

CHRIS JOHNSON My Mother at Fifty, 1974.

ROBERT LANGHAM Broom and Buckets, 1974. (Printed in Platinum).

NORMAN LOCKS Yosemite, 1974.

MARY ANN LYNCH Sunday Service, Kalapana Congregational, Hawaii 1974.

SALLY MANN Annie Dillard, Juggler, 1974.

ROBERT MINDEN The Hobby-Horse Riders, 1973.

ROGER MINICK Ozarks of Arkansas, 1970.

BOONE MORRISON Cinder Cone, Volcano, Hawaii 1974.

TED ORLAND Cemetary, near Hope, British Columbia, Canada 1974.

STEVE SZABO Church, Pokomoke, Maryland.

Winter 1975
FOR THE IMAGE CONTINUUM JOURNAL III

> *The only apparent solution is to postulate*
> *a new law of nature, to declare arbitrarily*
> *that the decay of mesons made of charmed*
> *quark and antiquark is inhibited by a factor*
> *of one thousand.*
> *Scientific American* Magazine

The Photographers' Equinox is close upon us, celebrating that magic moment between Winter & Summer when the cold water tap flows a pure 68 degrees. And bringing as well, here on the Monterey Peninsula, *Photographers' Weather*: a cloak of luminous low overcast that envelops the coastal ramparts for days on end. Photographers have been known to become entrapped in this light, not emerging for decades. Witness Edward Weston.

There is, of course, a *Scientific American* explanation for the weather. It tells me a great deal about the effects of thermal columns, cold water currents, vapor pressure, and the like. It tells me nothing at all about why a certain rock on Point Lobos becomes significant to a certain mind at a certain moment. My mind skips to Wynn Bullock's *Navigation Without Numbers*, peeling back layers of meaning not only to the subject in that picture, but also to the very process of creating it.

The real explanation, I think, is that Reality is grounded in Myth, not Measurement. Witness the weather, again: attacking with great mock ferocity, it wraps the Peninsula in wind and storm, until from our typically uninsulated California house we can almost hear timber wolves howling in the distance, or the crunching approach of a glacier inching its way down Chestnut Street. But all at 50 degrees, mind you. And as I drive down the coast, my red VW bus wobbling drunkenly in the gusts of ocean wind, and 30-foot waves rolling in against the rocks, I come upon Morley Baer's house wreathed in sunlight and the most glorious rainbow imaginable! There should be signs reading "*Scenic Turn-On!*"

And then there are the Butterflies, and the Whales. Great Grey Whales, commuting from Alaska to Mexico, rubbing up against the Monterey Peninsula as they turn the corner of California heading south. I watched four of them once, swimming single file a hundred yards away, spouting in unison and sounding with a flip of their tails. It was like watching a stoned freight train. Whales. And Butterflies. Monarch butterflies, returning to Pacific Grove each spring as predictably as the swallows return to Capistrano, drifting in by the tens of thousands—some days it's like walking through a soft orange blizzard. And I have this Theory (which has attracted a notable lack of converts, perhaps for lack of photographic evidence), that the *reason* they both arrive at the same time is because somewhere out (over?) in Monterey Bay, those whales and butterflies are *doing something* together!

Fast minds fog easily, I plead in self-defense. And yet each of us, saturated with input, construct our own matrix of Myth and Meaning to hold it all together. I've been looking through my photographs, and they tell me, quite clearly, that I live in a Mythical world—a world that gets along quite nicely without paying any great heed to the Laws defined so rigorously in scientific journals.

Over the past couple of years I've watched this world evolve photographically, from juxtapositions of opposites, to symbiotic pairings of the unlikely, and on to a point now where often a thing *is* its opposite. Concrete palm trees sprouting into freeways, flying people with mylar wings and aluminum bones, urban forests ready to relocate on a moment's notice—things like that. And others: images I don't really understand at all, yet keep returning to study on the proofsheet, unsettled by my own vision. And still others, too striking not to print, but still too dissimilar from all my other work to "Show."

Perhaps we all go through the same process, expanding our consciousness for awhile, then working out some means to present our new ideas. I remember visiting Boone Morrison in Hawaii a couple of years back, and being with him out on the volcano one day photographing a new flow of lava. Well, Boone would bound around this way and that—but, ah, *gingerly*, for the lava was still molten just below its thin new

palmus californai

crust—offering frequent exclamations to the Gods (along with numerous obscene if not downright scatological references to the fifteen-zone tonal range) and obviously enjoying himself immensely. But the moment he found a scene to photograph, he dutifully unpacked his view camera, planted the ritual tripod—and everything ground to a dead halt.

From that point on it was like watching Br'er Rabbit with his paws stuck in the Tar Baby: the West Coast Ansel Adams Workshop Graduate stuck making a one-second-at-f/32 fine-grain sharp-focus photograph, while the *real* Boone struggled desperately to pull free and chase a fleeting rainbow or the drifting mist over the next hilltop. And what was obvious was purely and simply that Boone did not lead a fine-grained life—certainly not one that ever held still for a full second!

Boone and I share a certain parallel evolution: for both of us technique was learned in advance of defining our personal vision. And a parallel problem: that our technique is increasingly working at cross purposes with our vision.

I still have a long way to go. I went to Yosemite this spring when there was to a full eclipse of the Moon. Though the Valley was crowded, perhaps only fifty or so made the pilgrimage up to Glacier Point, which remained blanketed by several feet of late spring snow. On that evening the sun still cast pink light on the distant High Sierra peaks long after the Valley had descended into deep purple shadow. It was a scene of wonder, the kind that sends tingles down your spine.

And later, when the last light had left, the Moon rose . . . and was slowly, slowly devoured by the Earth's shadow. All in total silence, until quite suddenly you were alone with all the stars visible on a moonless winter's night eight thousand feet up in the Heart of the Sierras.

Well. What does one do, then? I had a lens that knew only to resolve 100mm per inch, and clearly it was not equal to the task. Nor was I, being (as yet) unable to disengage the useless precision of an inherited technique. I made no photographs that evening. But, perhaps as a result, I did do a lot of thinking, some that has made it down into print here, and some that prophesizes new imagery further down the line . . .

November 1975

I WAS VISITING a friend today who owns a 35mm bulk-loader, and who was angry with herself because she had thought it was empty, opened it, and—LO!—you guessed it. So there were fifty feet of Plus-X on her kitchen table.

"Well," I told her cheerily, "go ahead and develop the film anyway. All the pictures you would have taken in the next six months are actually *already on* the film—running it through the camera is a mere formality." But alas, while processing it would have yielded a fine proof of the theory of pre-destination, she was equally pre-destined to view my whole idea as a gross affront to her Free Will. So it goes.

Still and all, there really are paradoxes—or at the least one hell of a lot of missing links—that confound our best efforts at matching artists' lives with their artwork. Edward Weston's

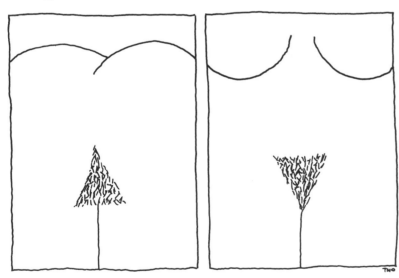

Ansel Adams & Edward Weston make very similar photographs.

images give no hint that he passionately embraced those women he photographed. And the amorous *Daybook* descriptions of his lovers are equally useless in predicting the neutral precision with which he would transmute them into classical studies of form.

And certainly *my* letters, though not exactly misleading, hardly offer a well-rounded view of my existence. Nor do my photographs. Still, I think I could reconstruct my life over the past few years with some fidelity from studying those images and writings together. And I wonder, could I have seen it all coming, seen the future revealed in the writing, revealed in the images, revealed in the interplay of the two? And even seeing it coming, could I have altered it? You can't have both Free Will *and* Predestination: having the former limits the latter to statistical probabilities—a decidedly uninspiring approach to eternity. (Reincarnation, in contrast, yields all kinds of possibilities: imagine Edward Weston out there *right now*, indulging his early soft-focus photography and soft-core porn life style . . . through reincarnation as David Hamilton!)

Spring 1976

WORKSHOP EVE. The class is filled, but the crowd that's coming, well . . . when I received the enrollment print-out, I commented to the people at UC Extension that I didn't spot any familiar alumni returning from earlier workshops.

"Oh," replied Vonna cheerily, "that's because we advertised it this time from a completely different mailing list: the Membership of the Photographic Society of America!"

Holy Bounce Flash! A whole salonful of artographers! Let's see . . . if I place the shadow of the bearskin rug on Zone III and the baby's face on Zone VI, then I can paint a sparkly Zone IX catch-light into the eyes. Now if I can just find some pink pebble-board . . .

[A WEEK LATER] For awhile, it looked like I might get a last-minute reprieve, of sorts: while I was on the road to Yosemite, a bee flew in the bus window, landed on my neck—*and stung me!* Last time I got a bee-sting, my leg swelled to

elephantine proportions and I was told I had developed a progressive allergic reaction—that *next* time it happened I would die within three minutes.

Well, "next time" having arrived, and being forty miles from nowhere, there wasn't much to do but sit back and count to 180, while trying to appreciate the sensations of my last three minutes. As it turned out, the main sensation—indeed the only one—was that the sting hurt like hell. It was almost disappointing—I kind of like the idea of there being a wild card in the deck, so to speak, that could eliminate me at any random moment. I guess the gods don't intend to let me off that easily . . .

After that encounter, the rest of the weekend was a piece

o'cake—turned out those PSAer's were all genuinely nice people, and Yosemite itself favored us with the best weather of the year: fancy clouds, a sprinkle of rain, no mosquitoes, the waterfalls running at full tilt, and even a full moon.

Better yet, Dave Bohn, who is becoming downright gregarious, joined Al Weber & me at the campground for the weekend. Turns out that Bohn *owns* Darius Kinsey's turn-of-the-century 5 x 7 STEREO camera, and though Dave doesn't know it yet, he's going to lend me that camera—I want to make a set of stereos of my own, complete with ornate stampings on the verso proclaiming:

Scenes of Wonder & Curiosity
T. Orland, Photog.

Summer 1976

SO I ARRIVED at Volcano town (elev. 4000, pop. 260) via Glenwood (annual rainfall 380 inches) after landing at Hilo (biggest city on the Island: pop. 20,000) following five hours of cloud-watching from a 747. Boone trundled down to meet me in his '58 VW bus (a veritable rolling filmbox, painted Kodak Yellow, with *Panatomic-X* inscribed across the back!). He brought along an unopened package that turned out to contain copies of *IC Journal III* arriving from Bayles—a good omen, methinks.

So, however unprepared, I've got my first Artist in Residency: a summer in the heart of Volcanoes National Park. I'm writing from the small cabin the Art Center has given me; it sits a virtual frisbee throw from the rim of Kilauea, though the locals cheerfully reassure me the lava always flows the *other* direction. Either way, I love the thought of the future laying right outside my front door!

Unfortunately, it only took me about two days to discover that immersing oneself in the local happenings has literal overtones to it here—I'm presently zonked out on aspirin, Contac and vitamin C, fighting a cold brought on by blithely walking through the pleasantly *warm* rain the day I arrived.

But as I sit here I have just had two visitors, each bringing something to help me escape my physical misery: Marsha Isoshima, Boone's Number One friend for the past two or three years, bringing home-made bread, and one of the students who will join our hike tomorrow—a beautiful Chinese girl by the name of (would you believe) Heidi Ho—bringing me a little packet containing an unidentified Oriental folk remedy. (Two packets, actually, because "you *beeg* person.")

And amongst neighborhood people, I must mention Richard (I doubt anyone knows his last name), the person around whom most all life revolves here in Volcano. Richard runs Hongo's Store . . . hmmm, maybe it's Richard *Hongo*, thinks Ted as a flash of logic momentarily pierces his foggy mind . . . well anyway, Hongo's is the only store in Volcano, stocked with everything from home-made sushi to baseball bats, and doubling as Post Office and gas station for good measure. Richard keeps the prices of everything in his head (which is

just as well, since they're astronomical: *e.g.* bread costs $1.20 a loaf!), writes them down longhand as you bring them up to the counter, and if you wish simply notes down the total so you can pay later when you have money with you.

The point is that Hongo's Store is a part of the process—in Carmel I can be a recluse, go out and buy food at Safeway anonymously, and *still* remain a recluse; but here, though one might expect the place is *made* for hermits, there is in fact no way to avoid becoming part of the process, part of the community, each time you step out the door. And if you don't step out, well, chances are someone will drop by just to make sure you're OK . . .

June 1976

TWENTY MILES OF HIKING, six earthquakes, and a gigantic letter from you in the past week—where can I begin? Since last writing, my cold has been transformed into a deep suntan (well . . . sun*burn*)—this the result of our four-day expedition into the Ka'u Desert and beyond. (Soon there will be proof-sheets, but Boone's off-the-roof-into-the-tank water storage supply has fallen low since the rains stopped, and film developing is temporarily curtailed.)

Our trek carried us across ten miles of shoe-devouring lava fields to a small shelter cabin built long ago for just such wayfarers as we. The shelter itself is set in a large grassy meadow that affords a panoramic view of the ocean some eight miles distant (actually not an uncommon vista, the entire landscape here being comprised of vast lava slopes fanning out to the sea from the three volcanoes that gave birth to the island). Our particular campsite is called *Kipuka Pepeiau*, which translates from the Hawaiian as "the place where a certain variety of ear-shaped fungus grows on the sides of trees in an island of forest surrounded by a sea of lava." The Hawaiian language is, I am rapidly coming to appreciate, marvelously rich.

Hiking those long hours through great frozen earth movements gave us a unique appreciation for the forces that created this land. And left us dead-tired as well!—by twilight we had unrolled our sleeping bags and lay back, in time to spot a satellite or two, and later watch as the Milky Way and Southern Cross slowly appeared in all their equatorial splendor. All viewed from a point some twenty-five miles removed from the last electric light that might otherwise fog the negative space of that great night sky. Impressive.

Summer 1976

KAREN PORTEUS & I just tried climbing the four hundred foot mini-volcano that had been rumbling underfoot earlier (see *Rumbles, underfoot, p. 248*, as Bayles would say). And we never did get entirely to the top. Problem is that the top surface of lava flows here tend to form solidified lava "bubbles" anywhere from an inch to a foot thick, and it's a bit like walking on thin ice in that you can find yourself dropping through to the next layer *very unexpectedly*. Most of the time that's only mildly disconcerting, but in this case the cone is still hot enough that steam is constantly pouring through cracks in its outer surface, and having the bottom drop out from under you is not an inviting prospect. Still, it would be satisfying to reach the crest, and if it's not raining tomorrow I'm going to take another run at it.

June 1976

WELL, TOMORROW ARRIVED, looking deceptively clear when the alarm went off at 5:30 AM. At the end of the road, though, peering the half-mile or so to Mauna Ulu, low clouds still clung to everything. Last of the nighttime fog about to burn off in the morning sun, I told myself, and optimistically plunged in.

Previous ascent had been from the west, blowing steam and sulfur down upon us, so this time I circled around and began climbing the east face, with increasingly stiff wind and drizzle at my back. It was a long and physically miserable climb, and my efforts at photography were singularly abortive—the cable release broke, I had to hold the tripod down to keep it from blowing over, and the rising sulfur condensed in the mist to form dilute sulfuric acid that *instantly* corroded the tripod legs into permanent three-quarter extension.

I kept telling myself the clouds would lift when I reached the top—they didn't, but it was worth it anyway. There is no hint of what awaits you, none whatsoever, even when you are within ten feet of the summit. In fact, I thought I *had* reached the summit, and looking through the mist saw nothing of particular interest other than a jagged line of mountains in the distance to the west.

Unsuccessful (but sinus-clearing) first ascent

Summit of Mauna Ulu, with jagged mountains in distance

Now one does not walk around unnecessarily on active volcanoes, but finally I decided to climb the extra few feet to a pinnacle of sorts where I hoped to get a better view of the distant mountains. Understatement. Being tired and freezing and probably muddy-minded from breathing sulfur-laden air, it had not registered on me that there *aren't* any jagged mountain peaks in Hawaii.

And so as I came over the last little knob, I found myself staring straight down into a crater perhaps five hundred feet deep, and straight across to the "distant jagged peaks" that suddenly revealed themselves to be the mist-softened facing wall of the crater. It was—forgive the hyperbole—awesome. And more than a bit frightening, with 30–40 mph winds pushing from behind, and the sudden realization that my current vantage point was a multi-cracked slab of *overhanging* rock. It spooked me enough that I moved back several feet from the edge before making a record shot, even at the expense of losing the optimum perspective.

Camerawork done, I retreated hastily, with the distinct feeling that the gods had gone out of their way to protect me. Later, arriving back at the cabin, I made hot cocoa, peeled off my soaked clothes, and relaxed in a hot bath for a long, long time.

July 1976

WE'VE BEEN HAVING a fine time with [my son] Jon here, even making some excursions just for his benefit. Yesterday we drove down to the old plantation town of Kohala for dinner with one of the sugar mill workers.

Afterwards, he gave us a night-time tour of the mill itself—what an awesome, eerie, frightening place! I'm certain that when archaeologists unearth it a millennium from now, they will quite logically deduce that it must have served as some kind of vast sacrificial torture chamber: endless conveyer belts that dragged *something* through gigantic machinery to be chopped up, squeezed, crushed, shredded, and then boiled down to liquid for storage in monstrous vats. All this running twenty-four hours a day under bare-bulb lighting amid *deaf-*

ening noise in a sheet-metal building. It must have been a hundred degrees inside the plant at midnight, and so filled with the pungent odor of cane sugar and molasses that we gasped for air in places. I promise never to complain about the cost of sugar again!

Our other big family outing included Boone and Marsha and their four kids, plus me and Jon and Karen, for a weekend camping trip. Ahhh, the pains and pleasures of parenthood, taking five kids aged 6 to 11 backpacking along five miles of hot trail! My photographic discovery of that trip was that I'll never be a Robert Capa: we were resting in the forest at one point when suddenly, silently, out of *nowhere*, emerged five Oriental men in full camouflage battle fatigues, carrying M-16's! Entirely friendly, it turned out—they were hunting wild pig—but they so astonished and unnerved us we didn't even think to photograph them.

Another surprise, equally disconcerting, arrived in the middle of the night, when hordes of two-inch long cockroaches inexplicably began running over me like a rush-hour freeway. They would *skitter*—a very distinctive sound!—across my sleeping bag and, worse yet, occasionally take the off-ramp down INSIDE! Aarrgh! And you know, my Travel Brochure never mentioned *any* of this . . .

Looking toward Mauna Loa from our campsite

SEE PAGES 59–60 FOR IMAGES FROM THIS TRIP

July 1976

NEARLY FORTY ROLLS of 120 film have sprocketed their way through my camera since June—an amount somewhat in excess of my annual output in more normal times. Even printing flourishes, with a dozen new 11 x 14's, including some hand-colored with oil paints (which may take *forever* to dry in Volcano's humidity). The past couple of weeks in have been particularly rich, with Roger Minick flying over from the mainland to join us—Boone & Frank Salmoiraghi & Karen & me—for an around-the-island expedition. Boone rented a Beeg Chevy Van for the week, and we luxuriated in the decadent style and comfort only an American six-mile-per-gallon behemoth can offer, drifting along at a thoroughly UnAmerican pace (like 20 mph), and abandoning the highway altogether when intriguing side roads beckoned.

One such road led to Milolii, a tiny fishing village inhabited entirely by native (non-Caucasian) Hawaiians; this is the village Boone has been documenting on film for a couple of years now, with the spin-off benefit that he is accepted as a friend—rather than a *houle*—by everyone there.

We arrived late in the morning, and had been idly exploring the main street (i.e. the only street), joking with the kids and such, when one of the small outboard-powered fishing boats returned to the cove. And there, being towed behind the boat rather unwillingly, was an eight-foot marlin (swordfish) which fisherman Aki had subdued after an hour's battle using a *handline*!

Within minutes about half the village descended upon the scene and lifted the fish—weighing 300–500 pounds depending upon the judge—onto the rocks, where it was carved (with a hand-saw) into cubic-foot chunks and divided among all. We stayed close to Aki, who invited us back to his house for a delicious lunchtime barbecue of marlin-steak, rice, Olympia beer . . . and *Spam*!—the latter being a staple in the diet of those living in the many outlying spots here that lack electricity (and, hence, refrigeration).

Only later did I learn that while the fishermen of Milolii sell their smaller catches at the Hilo public market, they have no choice but to keep the large fish for themselves. The reason, sadly, is that even here in the mid-Pacific—three thousand miles from Minamata or Los Angeles—these great fish absorb so much mercury and lead from the open ocean that by the time they're full-grown they are too contaminated with toxic waste to be sold commercially.

July 1976

THERE IS ONLY ONE ROAD around the Big Island and each person must follow this road. The same view is offered to all, but what each sees—now that is another matter entirely. "You will have three minutes at the Halemaumau Turnout; please have your cameras ready," instructs the tour-bus driver, and a thousand three-minuters a day dutifully record the literal reality thus placed before them. All of them making snapshots of experiences they never quite had, as Boone so brilliantly understated it. They see the land (*click*) and the people (*click*), but what passes unseen is the interaction *between* the people and the land, and the deeper cultural and aesthetic reality it reflects.

But there it is, a thousand years of Hawaiian culture lying just beneath a thin veneer of Americana, waiting to emerge in a myriad of forms—architecture, customs, speech—if you have time to pause and look. There is an old Hawaiian saying that others quoted to me a number of times at odd moments and with greater than conversational intensity: "The Life of the Land is Preserved in Righteousness." It's taken me a long time to begin to understand what they mean.

The Life of the Land is Preserved in Righteousness. An odd saying—anachronistic—at first I thought it was a carry-over from some earlier time when Hawaiians were essentially pantheistic. And then one day I was out driving with Jack Lockwood, a scientist from the Volcano Observatory. As we drove, the far horizon was dominated by 13,600 foot Mauna Loa, one of the most active volcanoes in the world. There has been speculation of late that its next eruption will send lava flowing northward to engulf Hilo, and so the volcano is monitored very carefully for indications of activity.

Lockwood's job for the Observatory is to interpret the readouts from their million dollars' worth of monitoring equipment, and as we drove along he gave me an irrefutably convincing statistical prediction—spiked with data from seismographs, tilt-meters, gravity/magnetic variations and the like—for the time and location of the next eruption. I was really impressed, as I always am, by the ability of science to so neatly cleave the Free Will of man from the pre-destination of the physical universe. And then, just as I was thinking that, Jack added in all seriousness, "Of course we also have to consider the possibility that these indications are just a *feint*, and that she won't move that way at all".

Dead silence.

I was at a loss for thoughts, much less words. Here was Lockwood, the scientist *in charge* of understanding what the goddamn thing will do, saying that just perhaps the volcano is purposefully misleading us! The statement itself was mind-boggling enough, but what was really unbelievable was that the idea would ever even *occur* to a scientist.

Those with an excessive faith in *any* system are not well-suited to make discoveries, and scientists in particular often have a mental tunnel vision bounded on all sides by hard facts, experimentally verifiable. What I am trying to say is that I think it was an act of brilliance for Lockwood to even conceive an hypothesis that allowed for answers that fell outside the accepted framework of scientific thinking.

Yet at some deep level where Art and Science meet, the real discoveries—the great leaps forward—are almost always made by stepping off the predictable path of straight-line logic, and allowing a sort of lateral shift (to use Robert Pirsig's phrase) in our thinking. Stieglitz did not ask the logical and predictable question, "Should I expose the cloud at f/16," but rather asked, "What *else* is a cloud?" And when he did, *our* world was transformed! The answers you get depend upon the questions you ask, as they say, and Stieglitz asked good questions; so does Jack.

Time itself resolves many questions, but what do you do in the meantime, when you must reconcile an impossible statement with its unimpeachable source? It was as if I were assembling a jigsaw puzzle and had it all neatly put together

. . . only to discover I still had a bunch of pieces left over! It wasn't as if I'd done anything wrong, exactly, but what the hell should I do with the extra pieces? Pretend they're not "real"? That they belong in someone *else's* puzzle? That my neatly enclosed logical construction is incomplete?

Finding no solution in the days that followed, what at first seemed just odd came to be perplexing, and then downright disconcerting. The *Life* of the Land—an interaction between the people and the land that goes both ways?! My mind was jogged back to the question each time a small tremor rattled the silverware in my cabin.

Finally, I decided to pay a visit to Frank Salmoiraghi. Frank would include his images, I daresay, within that genre we attribute to "the concerned photographer"; his work includes, among other things, a stunning photo essay about a group that has been trying to prevent the military from using one of the small uninhabited islands in the Hawaiian chain as a practice bombing range. The military replies that they are harming nothing by the bombing, that indeed there is nothing there to harm—only empty land.

The protestors, however, are acting not from the predictable premises of pacifism or ecology or sociology, but rather in behalf of *the Land itself*, which they hold to have suffered from the bombings. And Frank, I learned, agreed with the protestors.

"Do you mean to say," I asked pointblank, "that the land *feels* those bombs, that the land actually *reacts*?"

Well now, Frank is a sensitive and humane artist, but he is also a pragmatic commercial photographer and a Professor at the University of Hawaii; so I asked my question and lay back, waiting for the inevitable intellectual backpeddling to begin—perhaps something about the perils of taking idiomatic speech literally, or the need to treat another's cultural heritage with respect, or something along that line.

"*Yes,*" he replied, "*the land knows.*"

(opposite page)

THE DEATH OF WEST COAST PHOTOGRAPHY: AN ALLEGORICAL PORTRAIT
Or: The Day The Verticals Converged!
1975

SELF-PORTRAIT
Death Valley, 1980

ELEPHANT CROSSING

1979

Tractus Constructivus
Archaeological Treasures of Northern California Series
1979

DEER XING
Interstate Landscape Series
1980

THE EXTRAORDINARILY LONG BUILDING
1975

ONE-AND-A-HALF DOMES
Yosemite 1975

FOREST, OREGON
Interstate Landscape Series
1980

THE BRIDGE BETWEEN OREGON AND WASHINGTON
1981

JILL AT PEACE
Ka'u Desert, Hawaii 1981

BIG FISH AT MILOLII
Hawaii 1976

(next page)
BOONE MORRISON & ROGER MINICK
Hawaii 1976

August 1976

A DRIZZILY AFTERNOON, but I'm in good spirits. Still, I know this letter before I write it; I know it will take hours, that I will do battle with each word, each sentence. I don't know why writing should be difficult for me—it all seems so easy viewed from a distance! But somehow my letters to you all too often turn out like Brahms' First Piano Concerto—vast, sprawling, disorganized, exploring a range of ideas just a bit beyond the composer's ability to control. And the heaviness that results is not at all what I intend; often I start out *elated* by some realization, some wordless understanding of the world around me, and then sink slowly into depression from the difficulty of trying to shape that understanding into a few dozen sentences.

So, this summer I explored an island, made many photographs, conversed late into the evenings, read everything from Zen parables to Hesse, and more. And at some point it all *jelled*, forming a matrix of understanding, of enlightenment, and leaving my spirit more at peace than it has been in a long, long time. But universal truths, words of wisdom?—nothing.

It should not be so; there should not be such scant middle ground between itemizations and conclusions. I marvel at Hesse—he takes a character through a lifetime of experiences, each very specific, yet interweaves them and draws out from each an underlying truth or universal human characteristic. But then, perhaps all that any of us can do is take our volume of experience and shape its essence into form with the best tool we have at hand—for Hesse that tool was words, for me, images. I try to convince myself of that, but without marked success.

I'll take one more pass at it. I want to start with an end-point and circle back upon a paradox. Carefully, with short sentences. The end-point is that moment when a multitude of experiences *fuse*, creating an understanding that is far greater than the sum of the parts. The paradox is that this understanding becomes less and less manageable when I try to reduce it to words. I have thought about this, about the way certainty emerges as doubt when set to type, and I think it need not

be so. After all, what right has the intellect to question the spirit, the very source upon which it draws its nourishment? (The nugget at the core of *Zen and the Art of Motorcycle Maintenance* is a question drawn from the Socratic Dialogues: *And what is Good, Phaedrus, and what is not Good: need we ask anyone to tell us these things?*)

No, I think what really happens is that these sudden moments of wordless revelation send shock waves to all corners of one's consciousness, triggering the *next* thousand questions to be asked, the next thousand ramifications to be understood. But what then follows is all too often an example of simple human frailty: the very excitement of the day that prompts me to write you has wearied and muddied my mind by evening—glimpses of distant truths are obscured by nearby doubts, ideas are distorted or abandoned for want of word or syntax, and it's all downhill from there . . .

August 1976

MEMORIES AND BELONGINGS lay scattered about my cabin, awaiting their allotted departure space in suitcase or camera bag. Last week was in some sense the close of summer, marked as it was by the Art Center Exhibit of work I've done these past weeks. Last week was also memorable for a final outing—an overnight expedition with Boone and Jack Lockwood, coinciding with last full moon of summer, and bringing with it a conjunction of the many elements I have been trying to describe since arriving here.

You have to visualize the people to understand the process. There is of course me, wild-eyed radical and temporary escapee from a sheltered suburban existence. And there is Boone, Hawaii's own Native Funk & Flash, sparking energy into a hundred self-initiated projects (like the Art Center) from which more timid souls draw *their* energy; and, above all, Boone the true believer in photography as an Art, and in the inviolability of Hawaii's cultural heritage. Like myself, he is out beyond his depth, though swept along by different currents.

And finally there is Jack, every bit as unlikely a caricature

Jack Lockwood with laser reflectors

Boone at base camp, Red Hill in distance

of reality as Boone, though with a different set of unlikelihoods. He is impossibly strong, carrying a pack containing everything from homemade wine and all the ingredients for a beef stroganoff dinner, to *lasers* for conducting field experiments—great scene as he grabbed his 60-lb pack, one-hand pressed it to the sky with a Sumo wrestler bonzai yell, let it drop back on his shoulders and set off across the lava field at a pace that left Boone and I panting in distant pursuit!

Our destination, some miles from the roadhead, was a small, long-dormant cinder cone that appears on only a few maps, and then only under the prosaic name "Red Hill" (about as common a place name in Hawaii as "Grass Valley" would be on the mainland). But it is positioned at a most significant point on the Island, for its crest marks the first point inland from which you can see Kilauea Volcano, and the first place volcano-side from which you have a clear view of the Pacific Ocean stretching to the southern horizon. Perhaps for that reason, a USGS Survey Marker presently graces its summit.

We arrived about noon, and Jack immediately bounded up the 300-foot cone (composed of innumerable chunks of bro-

ken lava) while Boone and I sat at its base reviving ourselves with instant coffee. He returned soon enough, saying that he had *removed* the USGS Marker so that our intentions would be understood as peaceful. *By whom?* I thought.

An hour later I understood, for as I reached the crest myself I was suddenly struck by an astonishing realization—that while the cone itself was a natural geological formation, the surface I was walking upon *had been constructed!* That it was, in fact, an ancient Hawaiian ceremonial site, its entire surface divided into carefully levelled low stone platforms; and, built into the inside lip of the cone itself, a perfectly inlaid stone platform measuring perhaps 15 x 30 feet, positioned such that it could only be viewed as some kind of altar.

Boone lay *Ti* leaves—a ceremonial act of goodwill—upon the platform, and once again I sensed what I can only describe as a kind of acceptance, among those who live in Hawaii, of separate but equal rational and non-rational realities—a kind of parity between the experiential and the experimental in which Myth *co-exists* with Measurement. We explored further, sharing theories about what it all might have been, and finally just sitting and staring at the terraced platforms.

Boone said, "It's strange—your mind can see what's here, but there's just no way to photograph it."

And I said, or thought, "Perhaps the energy level is too high to be focused and captured by our little machines."

Finally Boone folded up his tripod, shaking his head and saying, "There's just nothing you can do with it."

And I thought, or said, "Maybe it's more a question of what it wants to do with us."

And so mostly we just sat and looked.

Or, perhaps, waited.

The site at Red Hill, though known, has never been officially investigated. Jack says it's at least a thousand years old; he's a master at deductive reasoning, noting offhandedly that it must have been raining when the lava last flowed here a thousand years ago, because its outer crust is too thick to have cooled in air alone. As we sat there he spoke as well of other things he has found—of ancient trails traversing Mauna Loa at the ten thousand foot level, leading no-where, but constructed at immense physical effort and obviously *used*. And probably it all relates back in a general way to the era when the first peoples were migrating to Hawaii, following the stars three and a half thousand miles northward from Tahiti.

There are many stories of those early voyages—stories that were already Myths by the time Captain Cook "discovered" the Islands in the late 1700's, and were only later recognized as fact. And learning these things, it no longer seemed so unnatural that Jack Lockwood, using Red Hill to detect Kilauea's activity through laser measurements to the surrounding peaks, would share a bond with those who came to this spot a thousand years earlier for analogously the same reason: to watch the Volcano to the north for portents of its activity, and to sight down the star track to the south and perhaps light signal fires for the great seventy-foot canoes plying northward from Tahiti.

Later, as the sun set, and Jack was preparing a dinner feast for us, I climbed back alone to the crest and watched as the moon, lemon-green in a sky of saturated blue, rose above layers of multi-colored lava, the closest being blood-red and interspersed with vivid green trees. And much later we left the base camp once again and climbed back up in the bright moonlight—this time following an ancient lava channel we found that formed a smooth grassy path leading directly to the uppermost platform. It was midnight then; we sat for an hour or more on the circle of stones that surrounded the altar, just watching.

August 1976

WELL. PAUSE. DEEP BREATH. Back again in the Land of the Locust. The descent into (or out of) reality took three planes, and was as pervasively hilarious as can be allowed for while sitting in a cramped space for ten hours while nothing happens.

The first flight, from Hilo to Honolulu, required an Aloha Airlines FUNBIRD, painted nose to tail with pink flowers and inspiring about the same confidence as the old California PSA line with its passenger-initiated slogan *"Sweat and Swear with Southwest Air"* . . . I mean, can you trust an airline whose pilot comes on the intercom as you taxi down the runway and cheerily announces, "Hi, this is your *driver* speaking"? Well, he did drive me and the busload of Japanese tourists safely to Honolulu; there, following a two-hour layover, I joined two hundred American tourists (wearing funshirts painted with pink flowers) for the flight to the mainland.

And finally, after another two hours of excruciating boredom in the SF airport, I boarded a 727 bound for Santa Barbara with a cargo of, well, *California Girls*. I had forgotten. In the Islands there is your occasional stereotypical Polynesian beauty, but usually under fifteen years old, for after that the genes take over and the men expand to three or four hundred pounds and the women to similar proportions. But here!—a whole airplane full of UCSB-bound co-eds, each one sort of tall and sort of slim and sort of blond, and all with these high little breasts so exactly the same size and shape you could probably interchange them in some mix and match fashion and neither they nor anyone else would be the wiser . . .

Fall 1976

I'VE BEEN PRINTING constantly for a week now, letting the dishes pile up on the dining room table while pressing the kitchen sink into service as a print-washer. Afterwards I unwind in the late afternoon sun, and eventually bicycle down to the Carmel Valley Store for avocados & artichoke hearts & all those other Good Things with which to build giant dinner salads. I'd like to hold onto this schedule forever.

And in the midst of these sessions a Wonderful Thing Happened; I was staring at some little negative projected on the enlarging easel, and realized my mind had passed right through it to *the original scene*—manipulating *that* memory, without first "translating" the scene into Zones and paper grades! I was reminded of a time long ago as a student, when after laboriously translating Latin into English word by word for many weeks, I crossed some unseen boundary and found myself understanding Latin *directly*.

So now with printing, Ansel's familiar saying that "the negative is the score, the print is the performance" has acquired a whole new level of meaning. Printing becomes a dance, like *tai chi*, using light energy for phrasing the emotional emphasis *of the scene*, rather than for burning and dodging different areas *of the negative*.

====

September 1976

I'VE BEEN WRITING an article for Mary Ann Lynch's new magazine *Combinations*, but it's going nowhere fast. Problem is, as soon as I come up with one sentence I'm sure is right, it generates so many mutually contradictory ideas to follow it that I get totally immobilized by the possibilities.

So now I've got about fifty perfectly good sentences, each its own great self-contained thought, and none of them fit together! I'm thinking of developing a theory of literature that says that the most noble ideas (*e.g.* mine), like the noble gases (helium, neon, etc.), cannot be combined with anything at all. I shall name these irreducible idea-quanta *Nuggets*. Facts, being of lesser value than ideas, shall be called *Flecks* (and those that have proven genuine and acquired devoted followers will be called *Genuflecks*). I myself, holding decidedly pes-

simistic ideas about human nature, belong to the heretical school of *Negativenuggetivism*.

According to the Many Words theory of Quantum Literature, however, the universe is constantly branching into a nearly-infinite number of different literary worlds, each inhabiting its own dimension, so that all possible writings constantly exist. It's comforting to think that somewhere Out There exist worlds identical to ours, except that in each a different Ted O. is pursuing a different one of the fifty possibilities that follow the first sentence of this letter. Just think, if you lived in the proper dimension, I could right now be leading you to profound revelations! Unfortunately for you, however, the Ted O. in this particular dimension has decided to chuck it all and go to bed.

====

January 1977

MUSIC. IDEAS. PICTURE the mind as a matrix filled with an incredible multitude of individual bits of sensory data, and one's personal world-view as a manifestation of the way those bits are interconnected. It follows, then, that a creative act (in any medium) requires both a passive openness to the rearrangement of those bits of data, and a discipline—an ordering principle—that will carry each rearrangement, each addition of new data to the matrix, to a higher order of coherence.

Of course there are lots of ways to loosen the connections—with alcohol, drugs, etc.—but they're generally useless, since they merely dismantle the existing structure of understanding without offering any new ordering in its place. But *music!*—music fills my mind with a latticework of pure structure, imposing an order—providing the instructions?—upon which my thoughts become organized with increased clarity.

At its extremes, music is the artform most capable of celebrating the joy of pure structure, and photography the artform most capable of recreating the world with visual fidelity. Do photographers suffer from a surfeit of substance—trees, relatives, sunsets, products, you-name-its—and musicians from the total absence of same? Is it some sense that either world, taken alone, is not entirely complete that lures so many musicians into photography?

T. Orland's Compendium of

PHOTOGRAPHIC TRUTHS

Being a Sampler of Morals, Axioms & Precepts To Which
EVERY PHOTOGRAPHER SHOULD EXPOSE HIMSELF.

The best scenic turnouts are clearly designated by highway signs reading **No Stopping Anytime**.

Edward Steichen owned a three-legged dog, which he named **Tripod**.   The Post Office folds all parcels containing photographs.

Camera straps never fail above soft surfaces.   Lens caps and cable releases can become invisible at will.   Dense negatives sink.

Shutterbugs result from cross-breeding silverfish with flashbulbs.   Spotone bottles are designed to tip over when the cap is removed.

Photographers fade faster than photographs.

Financial success in photography is directly related to proper choice of subject matter. Falling airplanes, exploding volcanoes, and certain Presidential motorcades work best.

Some Famous Photographic Couples: Polly Contrast and H.C. Won Ton, the Micro Doll and the Metro Gnome, Lynn Hoff and his Dear Dorff.

No two lightmeters agree.   A good photograph cannot be made in Fresno.   You will never, **ever**, receive an N.E.A. Grant.

The word "Daguerreotype" cannot be spelled correctly.   A new Hasselblad would take better pictures than your present camera.

1/60 at f/8 is the correct exposure for **all** photographs.

When your friends finally realize that you are a true artist, committed to making sensitive and meaningful images, they will ask you to photograph their wedding.

The most difficult problem encountered in designing the Polaroid SX-70 camera was not to get it to regurgitate a picture instantly, but to get it to make the appropriate sound—Bleaaagh!—when doing so.

Color slide viewing cures insomnia.   On any tripod, only two legs work properly.   Dust spots are attracted to sky areas.

Popular Photography is to Photography as **The Sound of Music** is to Music.   All B&W pictures eventually fade into full color.

Yes, Photographers Do It In The Dark . . . but they have to stop every thirty seconds to agitate the developer.

Distant objects cannot be recorded with short exposures—light travels only 186 miles in 1/1000th second.

Followers of Minor White are known as minor Whites.   There's nothing wrong with a 35mm that a 4×5 can't cure.

Ansel Adams has three Secret Zones known only to him!

Mountboard becomes stiffer by plying with itself.   When Man creates a sharper lens, Nature will create a fuzzier subject.

Safelights aren't. Available light won't be. On the other hand, gadget bags are.   Fast films compensate for slow photographers.

When the price of silver hits $76 an ounce, all photographs will be melted down for their silver content.

Owning more than one lens assures that you will always have the wrong lens on the camera for any given picture.

Mounting a photograph is a misdemeanor in Arkansas.

A butter knife is a useful tool for making minor adjustments that a camera store would charge $10 to make.

A camera store will charge $75 to repair a camera that has been adjusted with a butter knife.

Short exposures may cause reciprocity success.   Falling lenses are attracted to rocks.   Into every life a little grain must fall.

Sharper lenses won't help—realism is unrelated to Reality.   Expose for the secrets, develop for the surprises!

AND REMEMBER: Silver salts are sensitive to **thought**.

February 1977

FOR SHEER OPULENCE—we won't discuss taste—it would be hard to match the 75th birthday extravaganza thrust upon Ansel last evening at the Pebble Beach Country Club. The main event included an umpteen course dinner launched with stuffed artichokes, shrimp salad and other exotics, followed by a buffet of Poached Salmon, Stuffed Breast of Veal, Beef Wellington, Lobster, Bay Prawns, Cracked Dungeness Crab, Roast New York Strip, and Roast Leg of Lamb, and eventually culminating with a 40 x 60" birthday cake decorated in a mocha frosting facsimile of *Moonrise, Hernandez*. All arranged around a 16 x 20 camera *carved from ice*. Verily, Thorstein Veblen would be proud to see his Theory of Conspicuous Consumption so dramatically vindicated!

But Ansel endured the hoopla with charm and wit, accepting with gracious equanimity the praise of friends and the self-serving toasts of business jackals alike. And happily, I was able to come by Ansel & Virginia's for a private celebration beforehand, and presented him then with a print of *One-and-a-Half-Domes*—Ansel was delighted! So was I!

March 1977

YES GANG, IT'S TIME once again for the Friends of Photography's Annual Board Meeting and Bloodletting Festival. Not that they don't do it with class, including three days of *great* dinners, beginning at Director Jim Enyeart's house with a cast of seventy anointed taste-makers, money-makers, and even a respectable number of artists. Things got off to an unintentionally hilarious start at my expense when I overheard—and misinterpreted—a cocktail party conversation, and asked one of its participants if he was entrepreneur Harry Lunn . . . well, no, he was *John Szarkowski*, and he nearly choked on his drink laughing at the thought.

Over the course of the weekend I came to really appreciate Szarkowski for his gentle charm and slightly self-deprecating sense of humor—a refreshing contrast to the pompous vindictiveness of Peter Bunnell. I apparently ruffled Bunnell's feathers at the very outset by asking him about the list of nominees

he was submitting to the Board this year. (Peter is Chairman of the Nominations Committee, which conveniently picked exactly twenty nominees for the twenty open positions on the Board, and announced them as an apparent *fait accompli* a week before the meeting).

Anyway, I pointed out to him that the stated criteria for nomination to the Board is to increase the diversity and breadth of input into the decision-making process, and that his twenty selections included not a single minority, and only one woman. Then I said—*ahh, such naivety!*—that Rogier Gregoire (from Polaroid) and Anita Mozley (from the Stanford Art Museum) were both highly qualified and that I hoped to nominate them, both to give us a *choice* of good people, and to add a black and another woman to the list.

Well, I sure learned fast at the Board Meeting the next morning what it's like to walk in from the sandlot and find the Big Kids playing hardball—came time for nominations and Peter announced that "as a ruling of the Chair" it would require a majority vote to even *nominate* anyone other than his choices! For good measure, he added that a majority vote would be required to even challenge *that* ruling. And with that, the Parliamentary Express roared right on through before most people even heard the whistle.

Worse yet, he tried backing the train up over me again the next day. The occasion this time was the Friends afternoon symposium "on the current problems, needs and trends of Photographic Publishing." The panel consisted of Szarkowski, Jim Alinder (*Exposure* Magazine) and Nathon Lyons (*Afterimage*), with Jim Enyeart as moderator. The presentations were fascinating, especially Nathon Lyons for his exposition of the philosophical underpinnings of *Afterimage*.

During the discussion period that followed, however, I raised what seemed to me the fairly innocuous point that the panelists all represented the accepted "middle ground" of photographic publishing which the audience already knew and felt an easy rapport with—that essentially we were "talking to ourselves." Then I suggested that it would have been a good thing to include some heretics like Jim Hughes (Editor of *Popular Photography*) from the mass-media, or Ev Thomas

(*Bombay Duck*) from the underground press, so as to represent a wider spectrum of photographic publishing.

I had directed that observation toward Enyeart, who offered in return a short rationale for his choice of panelists—sort of a where-do-you-stop-if-you-open-the-floodgates type argument; then, surprisingly, he started praising the contribution we've made through *The Image Continuum Journal*—AT WHICH POINT Bunnell (who was sitting in the audience) jumped up and launched into this incredibly vitriolic diatribe, stating categorically that there is no need to include *anyone* from the popular or underground press because "every one of those publications is simply the beginnings of another *Afterimage* or *Aperture*, and *wants* to become another *Afterimage* or *Aperture*, if only it had more time or money to become one"—that there is no alternative to *Aperture*, only incipient or unsuccessful attempts to duplicate it!

April 1977

RUDOLF ARNHEIM & FRITJOF CAPRA, two wonderfully articulate scientists, both lectured here recently; and later, when I let my mind play with the ideas they presented, I unexpectedly found myself developing a theory about the nature of the bonding force between individuals.

Capra gave an overview of theoretical physics, beginning with a description of Heisenberg's Uncertainty Principle (i.e. that you cannot know both where a particle is, *and* where it *is going*). That's old stuff now, but what he went on to say was that not only has the Uncertainty Principle long since been validated, but also that it is now possible to prove that you cannot prove (got that?) that any specific particle exists at any given moment at all (!)—that things do not, in fact, *exist*, but rather exhibit at any given moment a *tendency* to exist or a *tendency* to disintegrate . . . that particles are in reality *processes*, non-existent except as patterns of greater or diminished coherence they display in conjunction with other particles (processes).

Arnheim, for his part, talked about the reality of a work of art—about how the scientist adapts his imagination to match the data recorded by his senses and instruments, while the artist accepts his imagination, and projects that reality outward through his artwork. Viewed that way, you can set up a hierarchy something like this:

Outer Reality

data
ideas
dreams
myths

Inner Reality

Well now, suppose that we can indeed work outward through myths and dreams to create new outer realities, just as we passively allow ourselves to be impressed with sensory data to form new inner realities. If that is so, there may be another whole realm, way below the conscious level, filled with worlds that have a *tendency* to exist, and surface in coherent form only in those moments when we bond with special individuals whose own preconscious worlds are complementary to our own . . .

April 1977

THANKS TO THE BENEVOLENCE (or naivety) of UC Extension, Al Weber, Tom Millea and I were invited to give a workshop in Santa Barbara last weekend. We decided for economy's sake to drive south together in Al's vintage Volvo. Things did not appear to be off to an auspicious start when we all hopped in the car, turned the key in the ignition and the engine responded with "   ". It was then, however, that I realized we were marching to the tune of a very different drummer (so to speak), for Al nonchalantly opened the hood, carefully scrutinized the precision machinery, gently picked up a huge monkey wrench, and went WHAP! WHAP! WHAP! WHAP! WHAP! on the engine head. Whereupon it dutifully started.

Murphy's Law is persistent, however, and some hours later

in the suburbs of Southern California El Volvo suddenly lost all power and rolled feebly to a halt, its engine still idling, the victim of a broken accelerator cable. Undaunted—and with a party arranged in our honor by one of Al's students beckoning twenty miles ahead—we attached a rope to wherever-it-is-the-accelerator-cable-goes, and with me tugging on the new throttle while Al steered and shouted "FASTER!SLOWER!" as occasion demanded, lurched fearlessly into Santa Barbara. Surely the phrase *"Hi Ho, Silver"* must have been coined by a photographer . . .

August 1977

LET THE RECORD SHOW that last night this innocent photog. was lured out at midnight and seduced on the Carmel Beach by A Very Well-Known Woman Photographer. (Which reminds me of the story—perhaps apocryphal—that Ruth Bernhard, when asked by a young follower just what Edward Weston was *really* like, replied, "Best lay I ever had!") I see a whole new field of research opening for photo-history graduate students . . .

Early January 1978

THE CLOSE OF CHRISTMAS holidays is at hand. As usual my calendar is covered with graffiti recounting the month's small achievements and disasters, though I'm not sure to what purpose. I somehow suspect that our lives must all appear remarkably similar at the day-to-day level—buffeted by random events while just trying to survive as best we can. What is it then that history judges us for? Making headway in a sea of Brownian movement? Stringing together the events of our life in some particular fashion? Or just being handed better cards by the luck of the draw?

For myself, I've always admired that wonderful passage from the ninth century writings of the Venerable Bede, describing the scene at a Great Feasting Hall in the north of England: it is winter and a storm rages outside, while inside the assembled Lords surround themselves with warmth and light. The Great Hall has but two small windows, one at each end of the structure—then, suddenly, a tiny sparrow flies in one of those windows, traverses the length of the Hall, and disappears out through the other. And Bede asks: are we not all like that sparrow, entering this life from some unknown place, fleetingly tasting the warmth and light, and disappearing once again into the blackness?

Summer 1978

A SUMMER IN THE SIERRAS, Vol. 1, No. 1, as they say. On the road at 4 AM, pausing once for coffee, and once more at sunrise to survey a hundred metal pyramids strung out like bizarre anti-tank emplacements across a dry riverbed. Even more bizarre, as I entered Yosemite, were the clusters of hooded pilgrims—harbingers of Ansel's workshop—bowing reverently over black accordions, each photographing the dead tree stump in the Zone of his or her faith.

And among them, inexplicably astride boulders in the middle of the Merced River rapids, rode the unlikely duo of Roger Gregoire [from Polaroid] and John Szarkowski [from MOMA]. Far out! I paused long enough to join in an exercise suitable for publication in *The Snapshooters Guide to Artistic Incest:* J.S. photographing T.O. photographing R.G. Afterwards, Szarkowski asked me to critique his Polaroids and I told him—HA! REVENGE OF THE ARTIST!—that they were *crummy!* Well, *good-naturedly* crummy, you understand—no use endangering my 1997 Retrospective at MOMA!

But that was all last week; this week I'm working alone, and making *hundreds* of images! Before the trip, I agonized futilely over what equipment to bring, finally simply chucking everything I own into the bus—Veriwide, Graflex, 4 x 5, and my little Olympus for record shots. Now that I'm into it, curiously, I find I'm using that much-maligned 35mm to the virtual exclusion of all my "real" cameras—it just *feels* right to be circling the Valley on my bicycle, Olympus swinging from my neck, tripod strapped to my daypack. After all, if God created Yosemite, it is equally the case that tourists and government created Yosemite *National Park.*

The Zone System Shooting Range

June 1978

HAWAII II: THE WORKSHOP that looked so good I *enrolled* in it—four days in the heart of Volcanoes National Park with Boone, Frank Salmoiraghi, Linda Connor and Judy Dater . . . all for $60 *including room & board!* Boone met me at the landing strip in his multi-generational bus (each door and the ignition requiring separate keys, having been salvaged from different places) and we lurched off into the mist as Boone chain-smoked *pakalolo* (grass) to slow down his metabolism, while the six-volt windshield wipers—connected to the *twelve*-volt battery—went ZIPZIPZIPZIPZIP. That lean mixture of mellowness laced with speed was to prevail for the next week or more.

And oh, so much fun playing student!—being led blindfolded on Judy's Castanada-style field session, marvelling at Linda wielding her 8 x 10 more gracefully than I can handhold my SX-70, consuming prodigious amounts of spaghetti & wine at our communal dinners . . . and even sneaking away with a friend from our dormitory-style sleeping quarters (quaintly segregated into "Boys" and "Girls" wings) for clandestine midnight treats.

Afterwards, Boone hosted a post-workshop trip around the Island for me & Linda & Judy (and Judy's friend Sam Samore, who flew in from SF), offering a rare chance for us to share some personal time far removed from the "public" banter of teaching situations. It's strange, I had always pictured Judy as being soft on the outside, but hard as steel just beneath the surface; and I still think that's true—as far as it goes. But underneath *that*, I now sense an even softer and more vulnerable persona, one that feels the hurt and fear that comes with continually putting herself on the emotional line in her art. Linda is complex in different ways—more cerebral, perhaps—and harder to decipher. Or maybe just harder to socialize with—I seemed to make an ass of myself around her with discouraging frequency.

For the most part, though, it was a warm and easy-going caravan, including one idyllic day spent leaving no footprints but our own on an isolated South Seas beach, barbecuing fish at sunset, and still later listening to the nighttime surf. Before completely dissolving into romantic mush, however, I will add that this same beach sports cockroaches the size of *field mice*, which spend their day patiently climbing the overhanging coconut trees, from whence they launch themselves at dusk and FLITTER groundward, with the apparent intent of landing inside one's shirt collar! *Yowie!!* I'm not sure I'm ready for paradise.

Boone, however, was truly in his element. When we arrived at Milolii, he took up the hand-casting fishing net one of the villagers made for him, and instantly his mind was off to

Linda Connor

another world, far away. Indeed, it won't be long now: one day he will go down to one of those secluded Hawaiian fishing villages he loves so much, and not return. Judy and I stood at ocean's edge that night as he silently slipped out waist-deep, poised with the casting net, listening for the fish that come to the surface and skip across the water in the darkness.

"I know this scene," said Judy. "It's from an Edward Curtis photograph."

Verily. He is one of them: speaking their pidgin English,

Boone Morrison

playing slack-key guitar in an all-Hawaiian band, learning to survive from hunting and fishing alone, and—rarest of all tributes—accepted by the Hawaiians as one of their own. Oh, there are lots of people—especially *houles*—who are put off by his unabashed pzazz and bravado, and fail to understand that Boone has managed what no person since Father Damien has achieved: establishing a true bridge to the original Hawaiian culture. Boone is *Ishi in Two Worlds . . .* but heading the opposite direction.

Fall 1978
On the occasion of Sally Mann's husband being elected to the local city council:
DEAR CITY CONGRESSMAN LARRY,
Congratulations on taking over a City Council seat.

You don't know me but I worked real hard for your election. I Delivered over 300 votes to you from South Side precincts. I'm sure you will appreciate this, seeing as how there isn't no more than only 175 voters in that whole part of town.

But you hadn't ought to think I want anything from you just because I got you elected—I did that because of my civic duty as a public citizen. Oh by the way my brother-in-law Antonio, a respectable businessman, has a garbage collection business and would like to work with you. He specializes in dinky little towns like yours, and has some of the biggest Contracts in the state. Tony he sees to it not only your garbage gets picked up right, but also your garbage trucks don't crash or your sewage plant burn down like maybe happens if you hire the wrong company.

Tony will come visit you soon. He lives in Sicily, but he commutes. He is also very civic minded and puts cash in the right campaign funds where he has the Contract.

Well, Larsy, I'm sure we can do beautiful business together. And give that cutie-pie wife of yours with the fancy tits a squeeze for me, eh?

Your Most Humble and Obedient Servant,
Teddi Orlando
Respectable Businessman

SALLY MANN
1982

DAVID BAYLES IN HIS STUDIO
Eugene, Oregon
1979

LAWRIE BROWN
1983

MARTHA CASANAVE AT HOME
Monterey, California
1983

ROBERT HEINECKEN AT HOME
Los Angeles, California
1981

JERRY UELSMANN AT HOME
Gainesville, Florida
1980

STARCRAFT

Yosemite Valley Series

1978

EXFOLIATING GRANITE
Yosemite Valley Series
1978

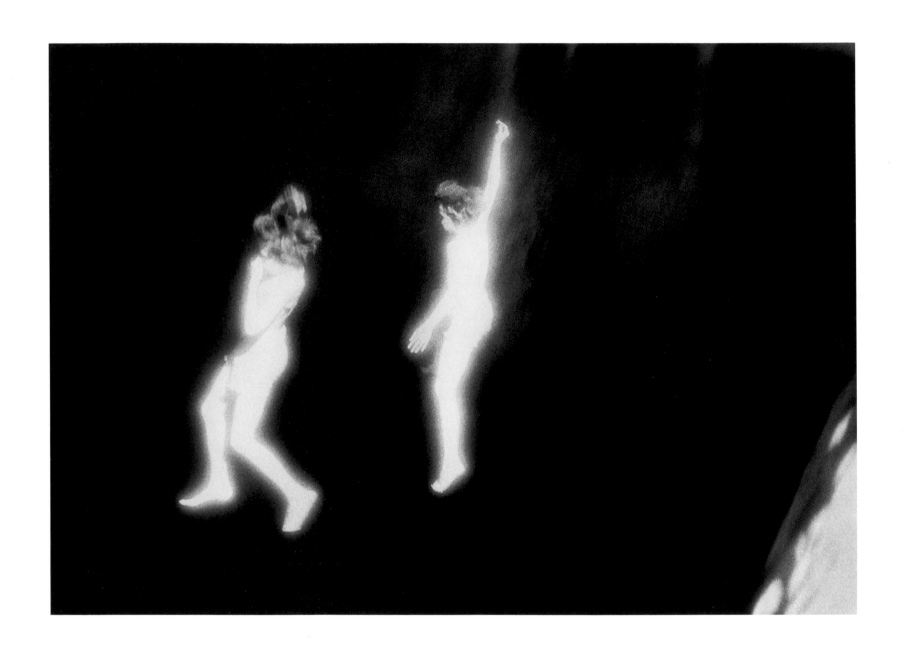

FALLING CHILDREN

Yosemite Valley Series

1978

September 1978

You've probably always wondered about the esoteric world of NEA Grants, about the lives of those distant, mythical figures who receive them. Wonder no more—I've just witnessed the process firsthand:

Seems the Walnut Creek Museum received money from NEA to undertake a photo survey of (naturally enough) Walnut Creek—enough money, in fact, to hire *two* photographers. So last week in came a phone call from said Museum, offering me $2,000 if I would work on the project together with . . . with . . . WITH . . . *Bill Owens!* Hoohah!! Verily, it's a thin line dividing the sublime from the ridiculous!

But then, *Why Not?*, Ted asked himself naively, and had no sooner asked the question than the phone rang and it was Owens himself, asking to speak with "Ben Orland." Hi Phil. He suggested that before meeting with the Museum people we get together for lunch and decide "what kind of exhibit we'll give them."

From here, words fail me. At least they did at lunch, which amounted to a priceless staccato monologue from the other side of the table.

Sample: "Well Tom, I think with 2,000 bucks we can put on a pretty snappy exhibit if we work it right, but for that kind of money I'm not gonna waste a lot of time—you artists waste too much time. First of all, the exhibit has to be in color—that's where the money is. Besides, color is the wave of the future; look at what the Museum of Modern Art exhibits: Stephen Shore—you heard of him?—and Eggleston and like that. They're *lousy* photographers but they get exhibited because they're shooting color. Besides, with color you can send it all out and don't have to—*Look at the tits on that waitress!*—go into the darkroom at all. . . . *I'm* not going into a darkroom for $2,000—it eats up too much time. I'll photograph families who live around here . . . I'll put an ad in the paper saying I'm looking for people to photograph—that's what I did with *Suburbia*—and let's see, if I do thirty families, that's sixty rolls of film at $7 a roll. Then I'll get 8x10 exhibit prints made—never make prints larger than 8x10: they get dented when you send them out for publication; it's dumb to make one set for exhibit and then have to make another for reproduction. Let's see, that's thirty pics at—*Look at the way they bounce when she walks! dubidy dubidy taptaptaptaptap*—$10 a print. Well, obviously they'll have to give us another thousand. We'll give them unmounted prints and they can mount them; it's hell trying to mount color—that's their problem. We can do the exhibit and then we'll get *Pop Photo Annual* to give us, say, twenty pages coverage. I'll get Joan Murray to come review it for *Artweek*."

But you know, for all that, my emotional response ran more toward empathy than outrage. He kept circling back to all the grants and teaching jobs he hasn't gotten, despite "doing all the right things"—sort of like a fish out of water, flopping around on the ground and wondering why he isn't making any headway in this strange (Art) environment. Not unlike the way I feel during my occasional, futile leaps into the business world.

May 1979
Catalog Statement for the Walnut Creek Show

My working approach to photography is absurdly simple: I wander around the countryside until I come upon something intriguing—then I reach for my camera. The wandering is accomplished in an old VW bus, and the camera I reach for is an even older *Veriwide 100*.

My research consisted of buying a roadmap of Contra Costa County. Then, during the fair-weather days of December and January I meandered along the obvious and the obscure roads of the Diablo Valley, adding about three thousand miles to my odometer, and averaging about three photographs a day along the way. The particulars of this involved leaving my Ben Lomond hermitage early enough to traverse San Jose before the rush-hour traffic coagulated to a standstill, and then sailing straight up Route 680 until I reached an as-yet-unexplored off-ramp. From there it was easy: I simply followed the path of the sun across the sky.

Now taking this approach to the Art can be chancy business when you have deadlines to meet, catalog entries to write.

After all, what if inspiration doesn't strike? What if your photographs remain obscure to *everyone*—even yourself? What then? Well, fortunately, those initial disaster fantasies always prove ill-founded later on when I circle back upon already-made images, watching as they slowly yield up their meaning to me.

And what I first sensed here was that the many objects cluttering my pictures were the very *least* important elements in the scene—that they were only the visible fragments of a deeper (but less tangible) reality common to all the scenes I photographed. It took several weeks to bring just that much understanding to consciousness, but soon afterwards, one morning at coffee, a whole cosmology tumbled clangorously and gloriously into place! Even now, that cosmology remains for me remarkably *visual*, only slightly abstracted by the tidy latticework of left-hemisphere thinking.

Picture, if you will, *change*—vast fundamental change, cascading in three great waves across the Diablo Valley. Picture these waves spanning several decades in time, moving at different speeds, crossing and mingling, setting up interference patterns, and only at rare points of intersection revealing clearly their source and destination. And label these waves: the natural landscape, the works of man, and the artificial landscape.

Of the natural landscape little remains, though a semi-domesticated version fenced off for cattle and tethered by hydroelectric wires is often proudly displayed in the distance on clear days. In most places, though, it is the second wave of man-made development that dominates, often so pervasively that only cars leave footprints, and even Walnut *Creek* becomes an architectural construct.

But even as this second wave sweeps over, depositing its layer of steel and cement sediment, a subtle but insistent undertow erodes its superficial permanence. Strange and groping, this third wave of change cuts perversely through the cityscape, carrying time backward toward a dimly sensed heritage. Here, memories are imperfectly transmuted, and the lost landscape is re-created in man's image, sowing Diablo Valley with neon palms and streetwise forests.

Trees XING

The images I have made here tell me these things; in time they will reveal more. Viewed closely, *any* scene is a hologram of the universe . . . it exists exactly as it does only because of *everything* that has come before, and all that follows will in turn emanate from what exists now. The inevitability of the future is as deeply embedded in the present as the irrevocability of the past. A photograph is a prophecy.

Spring 1979

ARCHAEOLOGICAL TREASURES OF NORTHERN CALIFORNIA
(NO. 3 IN A SERIES)
Mandible, tractus constructivus

CONVENTIONAL WISDOM has always held that the broad flat wasteland known today as greater downtown San Ramon is actually the remnant of an ancient alluvial floodplain emanating from the nearby Lafayette Sewage Control Plant. But as Lewis Binford pungently noted (in *Contemporary Ar-*

chaeology, p. 101), "We cannot afford to keep our theoretical heads buried in the sand," a warning that proved singularly apt when renewed septic activity recently sent flush floods tinkling across this desert, eroding strata to reveal surprising evidence that the plain had in fact originally been *constructed*. Primary evidence supporting this new theory was the discovery of a perfectly preserved *mandible* from the great prehistoric insect *tractus constructivus*.

Now the study of contemporary insects is gravely hampered by the fact that they are [A] teensy, and [B] liable to start CRAWLING ON YOU if you don't keep an eye on the little bastards! Happily, no such problems exist with *tractus constructivus*, since it is [A] extinct, and [B] big enough that paleobuggers (as insect archaeologists are called) can crawl all over *it*. And though the cause of its demise remains unknown, its unwieldy size doubtless made it easy prey for the opportunistic *hablis mobilis*, with its beetle-like outer shell and conservative lifestyle, and the nomadic *winnabagae*, which proliferated in spectacular locust-like fashion (and disappeared just as rapidly after outstripping their food supply).

However, the particular specimen whose *mandible* graces the accompanying Official Photograph was obviously pretty well off. From excavations at the site by stratigraphers, we deduce it was *tractus* itself which levelled the so-called floodplain, as a way of preparing the ground for its nest-building.

Having reduced the area to a monotonous flatland that predators would find aesthetically uninviting, it would then construct hundreds of elaborate—but absolutely identical—nests, building them from a yucky (*i.e.* from the Middle English *yech*, a vulgar term) substance called *ticky-tack*, which it secreted from its, uh, from its body. And into these tacky nests it placed hominids, rather in the manner that ants place aphids on leaves, to be periodically "milked" of everything they had accumulated.

Scientists were long baffled, however, because the number of technomic artifacts—Presto-logs, astroturf, pooper-scoopers, magnetic Have-A-Happy-Day talismans—unearthed at these paleostuccolithic middens indicated a larger population of hominids than could possibly have evolved at the site

through the process of Natural Seduction. The truth, as it emerged, was considerably more dramatic. (*than what?* ask sharp-eyed graduate students . . .) To wit: It is now known that many of the hominids associated with these sites did not live in the ticky-tack structures at all; rather, they spent their whole dreary life-cycle inside various species of *laundromata*, *vehicula toyotae*, and even *tractus* itself!

The entire story of this astonishing relationship is revealed in Lewis Thomas' childrens' fable, *Lives of a Cell*, cleverly disguised there as a description of the motile protozoan *mixotricha paradoxa*, which inhabit the stomachs of certain Australian termites. (Actually, the allegory is not all that highly disguised—I have known a number of people who rather blatantly resemble flagellating spirochetes!) The question we must ask is whether these protozoans, whose whole life is spent inside someone else's stomach, should be considered independent beings, or whether they are—as we view the *mitochondria* within us—simply a subsidiary part of a larger organism.

It is not a small thing to ask whether we operate from a condition of Free Will, Predestination, or Diminished Capacity, but in the case of *tractus constructivus* the answer is clear: that Great Insect is gone, yet the hominids once trapped inside continue to live! Yes, we now have triumphant living proof that the pre-Darwinian cosmology postulating *A Great Chain of Being* was essentially correct: that indeed all species *were* formed at The Creation, even though many were—and doubtless many more still are!—"bottled up" inside larger species and just waiting for the chance to escape.

This thrilling discovery serves as dramatic vindication of those protoscientists who long ago came so close to discovering the truth when they claimed that maggots sprang forth spontaneously from the bodies of decaying humans. Today we see that it was only their provincial, ptolemaic self-image that prevented them from understanding that the process actually works exactly the other way around:

Hominids are spontaneously generated
from decaying insects!

Spring 1979

ARCHAEOLOGICAL TREASURES OF
NORTHERN CALIFORNIA
(NO. 6 IN A SERIES)
Metatarsal, vehiculus rex

DIABLO VALLEY has yielded an archaeological wonder rivaling in importance the invention of *Piltdown Man*: a petrified metatarsal from the legendary prehistoric beast *vehiculus rex*! Site for this remarkable find is Oldavey Gorge, a popular wasteland formed by default (as it were) when the surrounding asphalt strata were uplifted during creation of the great chain of Safeway-Thrifties which still dominate the eastern horizon. It was during that eon, from the Late Plasticine to the Early Obsciene Period, that *vehiculus rex* ruled supreme (before eventually succumbing to the smaller but more agile *mopedia*).

Oldavey Gorge is named for Ol' Davey Damrosch, discoverer of *vehiculus rex*. Tragically, Ol' Davey himself was stricken with the dreaded Australopithecus' Revenge as he sat by his propane campfire sipping Campbell's Haldene Soup, and preparation of the Official Report of his discovery thus fell to his subordinates. "This unfortunate work, however, is so ill-executed in matters of chronology, judgement and information as to beg replacement by responsible scholarship." (Pretty classy sentence, eh?—I copied it verbatim from a dead-serious article in the California Historical Society *Quarterly*.)

But I digress. The wonder of archaeology is that with just a few bone chips or petrified bottle caps, plus some deductive reasoning, we can confidently tell you who ate who for breakfast a whole bunch of years ago. And logic being as it is, the fewer the clues, the more assured the conclusions. After all, any two bits of fragmentary evidence are likely to be contradictory, so the very best research results when only *one* piece of evidence exists. I modestly submit this Official Archaeological Photograph as *my* evidence.

In studying this picture, note that in the background we can see the tracks left by *rex* as it approached, with its metatar-

Metatarsal, vehiculus rex

sus marking the exact spot where it lost its foot(ing). Note also the tracks extending back underneath the large stone outcropping in the distance, beneath which *vehiculi* would gather, and with only their long snouts protruding from the darkness, and wait for unwitting *pedestria* to approach.

Significantly, many of the largest *vehiculi* evolved on the tip of their snouts a curious growth which took a shape "mimicking" the appearance of other species—often that of a luscious, nubile young hominid (sometimes with wings). In all likelihood, other hominids would be attracted to this "snout ornament," and when they got close enough, *vehiculus rex* would lunge forward, open its monstrous hinged front jaw, and *gobble 'em up!*

It was author Carl Sagan, in one of his longest leaps of speculative faith and most willing suspensions of disbelief, who so movingly validated this theory. In the unexpurgated Grove Press Edition of his fun story *The Dragons of Eden*, he writes, "Can we not but well imagine that the horror stories which mothers even today tell their daughters about the dangers of entering parked cars, are but a misty remembrance, still lurking in the R-complex of our *globus pallidus*, harkening back to that distant time when the relationship of parked *vehiculi* to getting eaten had *literal* overtones . . ."

August 1979

I HAVE THE PAST month laid out before me in Polaroid-a-day form, charmed by the way life slips so quickly and unexpectedly between matters large and small, and bemused by how difficult it is to tell—from a photograph—which events fall into which category. Our moments of genuine fear and passion and revelation are rarely visible; should I photograph a passage from a Beethoven concerto, a page from a book that sparks a childhood memory, a thank you smile from a sleepy friend?

If anything, the camera proves only the extent to which the world exists within our mind. If you did not recognize their faces, there would be little reason to separate a snapshot of

drinking buddies at the local bowling lanes from one of Hemingway & Durrell & Miller & Stein & Picasso sipping wine at some Left Bank cafe.

Juliana asked me the other night where I thought I was "in my career." I told her I was probably at the very peak of my productivity, but that the world was lagging about a decade back in recognizing the worth of my efforts. I was rather pleased with the latter part of that reply . . . until I began pondering the import of the former. If indeed this be the apogee, it is a frail and flimsy construction. I have, at best, seen a few fleeting glimpses of the universe, and captured almost none of them. Yet even in those rare glimpses I sense, just beyond my grasp, the meta-patterns that connect the patterns of a lifetime or a civilization.

Fall 1979

THE UPS PACKAGE propped so idly against my garage door today turned out to be my long-awaited *Stonehenge* print from Caponigro! So now, ringing the wall beside my desk as I type this, it joins my *Forest Angels* from Uelsmann, an equally magical Wynn Bullock landscape, the Weston of *Tina Singing*, your self-portrait, Dave Bohn's *Grizzly Bear*, and Timothy O'Sullivan's recording of *The Church at Santa Fe*.

In fact, the only prints that seem out of place here are my own! I fear the whimsical subject matter I employ to reveal the human condition may equally doom the artwork itself to be viewed as trivial. No matter how you cut it, the world will never take *Carnival of the Animals* as seriously as the *Ninth Symphony* . . .

Back home now, I've entered an Economic Free Fall Zone. It doesn't hurt, but then again I haven't hit bottom yet either. On the good side, I have a windfall profit to squander, the result of taking my small stack of early *Aperture* Magazines down to Weston Gallery. I was hoping to pawn them for maybe $75—and before I even got around to asking, they offered me SIX HUNDRED DOLLARS for them on the spot!!! Thank you, Minor White!

Fall 1979

In Appreciation of Jerry Uelsmann

ONE TRUTH IS INESCAPABLE: at some level all photographs are autobiographical. It can hardly be otherwise—after all, your camera rarely travels alone, rarely winks its shutter unless you're looking over its shoulder. Yet in the case of Jerry Uelsmann you still somehow expect that a line drawn between his life and his art will remain tenuous, abstract, intellectual—and probably dependent upon a future generation of art historians to decipher. *Not So*. After visiting Jerry on his home ground, I have a sobering realization to report: the man's life is as unlikely a composite of diversities as his photographs!

The sensation that I'd entered The Twilight Zone coincided with my arrival in Jerry's woodsy residential neighborhood, which curls gracefully and without apparent concern around a large communal pond. But, ah, the pond contains its own secrets, for as I approached I suddenly found myself under the sleepy, toothy gaze of a full grown *alligator* hovering transparently just below the water line . . . looking suspiciously like it had been *printed-in*. Life imitating art?

Jerry's home, camouflaged to pass as traditional west coast school architecture, holds other surprises once you step inside. To be precise, all hell breaks loose! Jerry's studio, which covers a fair proportion of the interior space, resembles nothing so much as some crowded basement storeroom of the

Smithsonian, with every available surface carpeted in fuzzy memorabilia from a thousand separate realities, stretching to all the corners and then unrestrainedly climbing the walls. Mickey Mouse telephones, McKinley for President posters, *Save the Chocolate Mousse* bumper stickers, extinct cameras, stuffed unicorns—fantasize it and you'll probably find it, lovingly placed in some carefully chosen niche. It's like walking around inside a Uelsmann photograph—I kept looking for the floating tree!

Jerry's darkroom is another exercise in eclecticism, rather reminiscent in overall ambience to the bridge from Captain Nemo's submarine, ornamented in nineteenth-century elegance with wall-to-wall carpeting below, and pervaded with music from an assembled multitude of hi-fi speakers above. It's also better equipped than most NYC camera stores, with an entire bank of matched enlargers hovering above matched easels and matched sundries. Rather than juggling negatives constantly, he simply sets up a different piece of his forthcoming picture in each enlarger, and then moves his printing paper on down the line, building up a latent image en route.

But while his darkroom houses the leading edge of Western technology, Jerry's personal belief system harbors a good-natured faith that the process is really, well, *magic*—an attitude he demonstrated in hilarious fashion for students at the Yosemite workshop by donning a homemade pointed Sorcerer's cap (festooned with fluorescent stars & comets!) while materializing a print for them.

There's a lot of showmanship in all that, of course, but at its source is a genuine playfulness that's liable to appear at any moment—like one evening after we'd consumed mucho pizza & wine, when Jerry plunked himself down at his player-piano, sporting a giant cigar in one hand and a *kazoo* in the other, and proceeded to accompany himself at full volume to the pedal-generated chords of Beethoven's *Ninth Symphony!* And it was a wonderful performance, filled with the exuberance of someone who reaches out to touch a plurality of worlds. The true richness of art, after all, derives from the fact that it is created by real people—what sets the Masters apart is not their greater godliness, but their greater humanity.

Jerry downs a floating tree!

October 1980

MY ANNUAL N.E.A. REJECTION SLIP arriveth today, and for solace I'm going to spend the evening processing trip pictures from last week's Oregon Workshop with David.

We stayed at an unused Coast Guard station adjacent to the absurdly picturesque but still functioning Heceta Head Lighthouse, spending our days grappling with the Monster (Photography as Art). And the evenings? Well, the Oregon coast is not only beautiful, but also marvelously lush and unpolluted—so for meals we gathered mussels from the beach and bright red lobsterlike crayfish from the freshwater streams, serving them steamed with melted butter. And wild blackberries for dessert. Yum!

As you might suspect, this overindulgence led directly into further festivities as the evening progressed. And/or to the Gen-u-ine Educational Experience of just sitting back and watching a *real* professional—*i.e.* Bayles—go to work.

There was, you see, this model, whom I'll call Liz (since that was her name). Liz is intelligent, attractive, unattached, and spent most of each day wandering among us naked. David, however, blithely ignored her entirely until our closing night party, at which point he took aim on her the way a cheetah singles out a lone gazelle . . . and after two hours of solid drinking and intense conversation—remarkable in itself for David's ability to maintain *unblinking* eye contact from inches away for minutes on end—closed upon his hypnotized quarry and carried her away into the night. *¡Olay!* In other cultures they could award him both ears and the tail.

(Moral Certitude, however, requires me to note that David spent the better part of the following morning munching aspirin and offering soliloquies on such topics as "Remorse.")

Seriously though, the chance to share hours of conversation with David made the whole trip worthwhile. His new work is provocative—vastly more successful, I think, than what emerged from his brief flirtation with 8x10 Polaroid montages. He did, however, get sucked into another group Portfolio this year—a highly polished but otherwise vacuous presentation by Susan Spiritus Gallery of about twenty photographers she

Relaxing with David Bayles at the Oregon Coast Workshop

represents at her Gallery. The extravaganza came boxed in a clear plexiglas case, with each print enclosed in a wrap-around sheet imprinted with the Gallery's idea of the artists' life history—Shows, NEA Grants, coffee-table books. All things considered, it was *very* ugly—I'll take our homemade *IC Journal* over it any day!

February 1980

CENSORED IN UTAH! An Historic First! Dana, spread-eagled at the base of *The Day the Verticals Converged*, was more than Mormon sensibilities could handle. Not to mention *Angels Doing It!* Things began to go amiss from the first phone call, when they offered to fly me out to give a lecture after the Opening, adding that they would be happy to have me bring "Mrs. Orland" with me.

"Well", I replied cheerily, "I'm kind of *in between* marriages right now, but there is someone else I'd love to bring."

Long frosty silence. Followed by: "I'm afraid the State of Utah doesn't cover the cost of a *travelling companion*."

Uh, right, I'm not sure my kid sister could make it anyway . . .

Utah Vignette: Reaction of local TV newscaster to actual news. A small plane had crashed at the edge of the city an hour earlier. The announcer says the mobile TV truck has just reached the scene. Cut to second newscaster standing in out-door field with blank background: "We're here with our cameras at the scene of the light plane crash. It's a horrible scene. It's really a terrible crash. Just awful. In fact it's *so* bad I'm not even going to let you see it. Now back to News Central." Cut from newsman to studio.

Utah Vignette II. Reaction of Utah State Photography Department to actual photography. When I told the head of the Department my choice for the $100 Purchase Award in the photo contest I juried for them, he replied, "Arazoo? (*wince*). Oh. Uh, yes, I know her. Does the best work at the university. Only been at it a year and a half. She's a *girl*. Only one we have. *Iranian*. And very—what's the word?—*assertive*."

I later met Arazoo. I told her I'd be happy if I could make prints as flawless as hers; without batting an eyelash, she replied, "I'll teach you." Keep your eye on that one!

June 1981

MY COLLECTION of Interstate Landscapes is growing by leaps and bounds, the latest leap (or bound) carrying me halfway to the North Pole—at least that's what the sign said as I passed the 45th Parallel somewhere in Oregon. Before money & energy gave out, I touched the Canadian border and circled back down the Olympic Peninsula.

And I have to admit there's something attractive—even seductive—about driving hundreds of miles along the In-terstate, always twenty feet or so above the surrounding land-scape. I think it has something to do with the way the land-scape has been altered to make way for the freeway; you glance out the side window and watch continuing lines of horizontal strata receding into the distance—from pavement to shoulder, then guard rail, edge cut or fill, boundary fence, phone poles, railroad tracks, frontage road, billboards and so on outward to the horizon.

Most of the time the elements clash and the message is garbled, but every now and then you intersect some magic point where this tension between urban and rural sensibilities has reached a clear visual resolution, an equilibrium point—and *those* views turn out to be almost dangerously beautiful.

The trip itself got its impetus from a phone call that roused me from a dead sleep one morning last week. Transcript:

"Hello, Mr. Orland? I'm calling to see if you're still in-terested in the job at Oregon."

"Job? Oregon? What?"

"At the University. In Eugene. You put your name in two years ago when we announced the position. The funding just came through and you're a finalist—would you like to be interviewed?"

"Me? Uh, sure. I guess so. When?"

And with that—LO!—on comes The Head Of The Art De-partment! Well, given that all this happened *sans* even a cup of coffee to raise my pulse to a detectable level, I haven't the *foggiest* remembrance of anything I said. But whatever it was, my dream state (or metabolism) apparently suits Oregon, because the next day they called back and offered me—sight unseen—an Assistant Professorship! Now why don't the jobs I *want* drop into place that easily . . . ?

July 1981

SUMMER IS SLIDING AWAY as inevitably as the San Andreas Fault; already the days seem shorter, if only because the mornings race past this late riser. In Santa Cruz they wear *Invasion of the Medfly* T-shirts; in Carmel it's green checkered golf pants. At Toot's Lagoon Restaurant, where Frances works, an invasion of Irish tourists raise their tenth round of drinks to toast "the Americans and their funny clothes." And here at the hermitage, clothes are dispensed with altogether at pool-side once the sun burns through the morning fog. Friends have been trooping over all week to bid their friend/ professor farewell as he prepares to disappear into oblivion (*Oblivion, Oregon 97405*). They bring wine & cheese & ice cream & home-made pies, and leave behind stacks of bittersweet Polaroid memories.

Soon even that will be ancient history—tomorrow, Frances & I head northward to find a new home. Together!

November 1981

COLOR AUTUMN RED. To pacify my wanderlust, I recently attended the NW regional SPE Conference in Spokane, mingling for two days with a hundred academic lifers. And discovered that a seeming near-majority of these photo-exiles to the western provinces are—ready?—honest-to-god(less) COMMUNISTS! Holy Monopoly!

Yes, at various Conference lectures I learned from them that the rest of us poor camera-bearing drudges are mere tools of the reactionary capitalist ruling class, dutifully cranking out visual propaganda for Sears Catalogs, Bank of Amerika Brochures, and R.O.T.C. Enlistment Posters.

But alas, while Photography-According-To-Marx offers at least an, uh, *imaginative* view of the world, that's more than can be said for its converts . . . your favorite fascist toadie found it difficult to listen without laughing as myriads of straw men were clumsily set up just for the (faintly decadent?) pleasure of whomping them into the ground with blunt ideology. I wish I'd brought the button Juliana gave me that reads *"Question Stupidity."*

January 1982

THERE'S SOMETHING STRANGE and frightening about the way your life trundles cheerfully and mindlessly along, while Death lingers just behind to stalk friends you had been casually talking with a short time before. So we concluded our California visit and crossed Siskiyou Pass into Oregon, as simultaneously three feet of rain fell on Ben Lomond, burying two of my best friends fifty feet beneath a sudden forest landslide. Frances & I had stayed at another friend's house just down the road from there two nights earlier, complaining all the while of Oregon's incessant drizzle.

The whimsy of the gods so often seems filled with such contradictions . . . I read recently that archaeologists had uncovered a twenty thousand year old religious site somewhere in Europe. Its prehistoric inhabitants had evolved far beyond the stage of simply burying their dead—by all indications they had a fully developed religion that included ritual

Frances Connolly

and symbolism, a belief in a god who watched over and pro-tected them, a belief in their future. The inhabitants were Neanderthals—*doomed*, every last one of them, to extinction. And yet (astonishingly) their cave art remains, reaching across time, even across *species*, trying to tell us something.

On that same trip we had had dinner Christmas night at Maggie Weston's in Carmel, joined by most of the Weston clan, Ansel & Virginia, and a handful of friends. And there, even while being pleasantly seduced by champagne and ca-tered service and all the other accoutrements of corporate wealth and blurred motives, my gaze drifted to the photo-graphs on the walls . . . *wondrous* photographs—a Weston *Pepper*, a Watkins Mammoth Plate, a Steichen gum print, Cameron's *Herschel*, a Stieglitz, and more—photographs sing-ing with almost painful beauty and intensity. I would count my life well spent if I were to produce *one image* that could touch another, someone from another time and place, as fully as those pieces reached out to me. I wonder if the maker of cave art ever harbored that same thought . . .

―――――――――――――――

November 1982

DEAR MRS. MANN,

Your government wants to assure you that President Reagan places the highest priority upon finding a woman recipient for an N.E.A. Award someday. We regret to inform you, however, that you are not among those being considered seriously this year to receive what is, after all, a *Fellow*ship.

Next year, however, you'll find it much easier to push that N.E.A. boulder up the mountainside, thanks to a newly-created "Girlship" Category! That's right! No more singing the "blues" from trying to prepare difficult artwork: now you can be judged instead for "flair & originality" in your answers to a few pages of simple, confidential questions about your Age, Personal Needs, Styling Secrets, Church Affiliation, Fa-vorite Recipes, and Stance on Abortion.

Because of the need to trim wasteful non-defense spending, these N.E.A. Girlships will not include any "pin money"; instead, winners will receive a handsome simulated-bronze charm bracelet bearing the likeness of Phyllis Schafly on one side, and John Wayne on verso.

We hope you will not be discouraged that the images you submitted this year were so inferior, and encourage you to compete at your own level in the future.

Your Official Application and Loyalty Oath Form will be sent upon receipt of your fifty dollar non-returnable Entry Fee.

> Yours Truly,
> Senator Strom Thurmond
> New Director
> National Endowment for the Arts

―――――――――――――――

March 1983

THE FLORA AND FAUNA in your life are intimidating in their complexity, Sally. You do realize, of course, that to keep your banana tree healthy and happy you'll need to import a boxful of banana *spiders*. But don't worry, they'll blend right in, and given their unbelievable size will be mistaken by un-wary guests as charming clockwork toys. Being furry as well, they're almost as lovable as toy poodles, and will give you unceasing pleasure as you slide toward grandmotherhood.

Here, we've been awaiting Spring for months. Oh, it's true that Frances' tulip bulbs are already sprouting beautifully . . . problem is they're sprouting *inside their plastic baggies*—the garden remains too waterlogged to plant them. I really felt sorry for the little things—even accused Frances of plant abuse, threatened to call the SPCP, etc.—but later at the local discount garden store I saw aisle upon aisle of the poor veggie critters sprouting the same way, wanly reaching for the fluo-rescent lights.

Doesn't surprise me—fluorescent's the closest thing to sun-light around. Earlier this winter Eugene had thirty-nine *con-secutive* days of rain. Not that that was a record, mind you. I know it wasn't because on the fortieth day, when it was *only* cloudy, the newspaper headline read, "Dry Day Ruins Try for Record"—they were unhappy because it *stopped* raining! Now *that's* sick!!

Monument to the Unknown Photographer

Spring 1983

CHALK UP ANOTHER awkward attempt at integrating Art with Reality, courtesy of this year's *Society For Photographic Education* Annual Conference. It was held in Colorado at the Broadmoor, a hotel of not inconsiderable pretensions, including five indoor swimming pools, indoor tennis courts, sauna, etc., and a simple payment policy of accepting only *their own* credit card (or hard cash). So there we were, a hotel full of starving photographers—some of us literally, since even a hamburger cost $8.00!—coming together to explore strategies in support of the Conference's theme topic of *Survival of the Artist/Teacher in the Present Era.* Ironic.

But in a strange way, that topic was addressed more directly than anyone expected. It began when Lou Stoumen, a humanist whose work has always closely reflected his life experiences, spoke about his recent trip to Japan. Before that, Lou had last been in Japan—well, *over* Japan—while flying B-29 raids in 1944–45. But now he showed slides of his return, nearly forty years later, to lay flowers at the memorial of a city he had once helped destroy. He spoke eloquently, passionately, of the lessons he has learned, the lessons all survivors learn.

A day later, in counterpoint to Lou's wisdom, the world grew curiouser and curiouser. I think I was among the first to notice the presence of a dozen tall, broad-shouldered Caucasian men wearing well-tailored (but oddly lumpy) business suits and tiny earphones. Secret Service. Soon military men began to appear, dressed in various nationalities of uniform, most sporting more stripes than you'd find on a zebra. And so it came to pass that even as S.P.E. members were packing to return home and fight another rear-guard action against budget cuts to education, the people who brought you Hiroshima and Vietnam were arriving to convene a NATO Defense Ministers Conference to discuss sending a few thousand more nuclear warheads to Europe.

It would not have bothered me to see them all lined up against a wall and shot.

Photographically speaking, of course.

The Eugene Ballet Company in rehearsal,
from a class project titled "Setting the Stage"

Spring 1983

AS A CLASS PROJECT, my Photographic Book class at U of O has been photographing the Eugene Opera, Symphony and Ballet companies in rehearsal. With a half-dozen superb students and David [Bayles] volunteering as an added guest instructor, the course has become a runaway success!

Better yet, our little group has become Eugene's *hot item*, receiving invitations to photograph guest stars and special performances at the new Performing Arts Center, offers of an end-of-term Show from Eugene's only real Art Gallery, and even about $4,000 in pledges from local art patrons to bankroll the book's publication.

You probably think the U of O Art Department would be ecstatic to see someone offering a class with actual *content*, one that reaches out to interact with the surrounding community, one that makes art a truly interdisciplinary process merging photography & writing & graphic design, one that motivates the students to work with such intensity.

Well, think again.

Picture an Art Department that hears of students in some *photography* class producing more (and better) graphic design work in two semesters than their dull (but tenured!) professors have turned out in the past two decades. Picture crumbling paper empires. Picture professional jealousy. Picture territoriality. Picture an Inquisition:

Dept: Is it true you were *selective*—that you applied *personal judgement*—in admitting students into this class?

Instr: I had fifty people wanting to enroll, so I reviewed their portfolios and admitted the best; it is, after all, a graduate class!

Dept: This is a STATE university—*you are not permitted to discriminate on the basis of quality.*

Dept: Is it true that you have been allowing outsiders into your classroom?

Instr: Well, students from other classes have taken to sneaking in to join our discussions; also, we've had David Bayles helping us, and the Directors and stars of the performing groups as guest speakers.

Dept: There is no Departmental budget for Guest Speakers.

Instr: They've all volunteered their time.

Dept: If someone is not been paid, then by Departmental definition he is not a Guest Speaker. And if he is not a Guest Speaker he cannot attend your class without first applying for admission to the University and paying tuition. *It is against Departmental Regulations to speak for free.*

Dept: Is it true that your students have been using the Darkroom more hours than the Department has allotted— that some have even been staying in the building and working *all night long?* That some even worked over *semester break,* when classes weren't even in session?!

Instr: Strange to have students *wanting* to work, isn't it?

Dept: *Departmental Regulations forbid students working on photography after 9 PM.*

Dept: Is it true that you have actually been *making photographs* along with the students at the field sessions?

Instr: Yes; they say it's a wonderful change to be around an actual working artist.

Dept: *You were hired to teach, not to make art.*

Well *sheee-it*. California is looking better all the time . . .

June 1984

IT FELT LIKE HOMECOMING, returning to the Yosemite Workshop with so many friends. At one point a student asked me how we arrived at our particular line-up of instructors; the answer, I suppose, is simply that ten years ago Ansel let me bring my friends on board as Assistants, and this year I got the chance to bring my friends on board as Instructors.

But when she asked the question I also had this sudden flash that another common denominator is that each of my friends has a keenly honed sense of humor. Highly idiosyncratic ones at that, ranging from bawdy (Uelsmann) to deadpan (Caponigro) to drier than a 6:1 martini (Dave Bohn).

Dave, as a matter of fact, consistently whistled lines right past the assembled crowd (and on occasion yours truly); *e.g.* I knew Dave wanted to deliver a eulogy for Ansel at Olmsted Point on our High Country fieldtrip, so when we got there I suggested we all climb a few hundred feet up the granite slopes to separate ourselves from the tourists.

"What?" he responded with utter disbelief. "You mean, carry the P.A. equipment all the way up *there*?"

Zing. Took me half a minute.

I even go for the bait when he's *serious.* At the opening of his evening lecture he allowed as how he hadn't given this talk before and wasn't sure how long it would take, but was fairly confident it would run between 37 and 37:25 minutes.

This time I've got him!, I thought, as I secretly activated my stopwatch. It ran 37:05.

Later, confessing my machinations to him, I think I caught the faintest upward crinkle at the edge of his lips.

AFTERWORD

THE IDEA FOR THIS BOOK arose about the time I returned home to California in 1984—a move that brought closure (more gently than I probably deserved) to an era of my life. Somewhere in the course of that decade, imperceptibly, I had become a photographer. And while it's taken yet another few years to bring this book to print, it still feels right to close the entries with that Yosemite letter.

That editorial grace period yielded other benefits as well. In the course of re-reading my early letters, I suddenly knew what Edward Weston must have felt that led him to preface his *Daybooks* with those painfully honest words, "How young I was." Looking back now—at myself, at Sally, at my friends from the *Image Continuum*—I marvel at all the laughter and tears, all the youthful fervor and sincerity we lavished upon testing the strength of our ideals against the rules of the system. It was all incredibly naive, of course, but even now I'm not sure I'd change much of anything.

Nor would the others, I suspect. Witness that early snapshot (*page 6*) of our gathering in Yosemite, sporting between us not a single exhibit or published work, just waiting for the future to happen. Now hit the Fast Forward button.

David Bayles is today an Instructor at those same Yosemite Workshops, as well as an expert guide in whitewater rafting and steelhead fishing. Boone Morrison founded the Volcano Arts Center a year after that group picture was taken, and a decade later has branched into self-publishing and architectural design as well. Chris Johnson took up teaching and now heads the Photography Department at California College of Arts and Crafts, while Robert Langham went on to study journalism and is now a crack photo-journalist in Texas.

Meanwhile, Sally Mann has done just about everything, along the way garnering Fellowships from the National Endowment for the Arts, the Guggenheim Foundation and the Friends of Photography, monographs of her work published by David Godine and Aperture, and inclusion in most major museum collections across the country.

The Image Continuum Journal itself, which brought so many good photographers—famous and otherwise—together as friends and equals, served its purpose well and has been dormant since 1981, patiently awaiting its next incarnation.

And as for myself, well, perhaps one benefit of testing the boundaries of my life has been simply to carve out some extra maneuvering room on down the line. I sense very clearly that my photography is not building toward some grand Wagnerian climax, but in trade I've found a real freedom in letting my images explore the world like some uncharted stream, hitting a few unexpected rapids here, a quiet deepwater pool there, and generally carrying me into enough surprising and unexplored territory to keep life interesting. It's all a matter of perspective: you just have to keep your eye on the far horizon . . .

T.N.O., *Spring 1988*

DAWN FROM THE CREST OF THE SIERRA NEVADA
Mono Pass, Yosemite National Park
1987

GATES OF THE VALLEY
Yosemite National Park
1984

MERCED RIVER, WINTER
Yosemite Valley
1985

MAMMOTH HOT SPRINGS, WINTER
Yellowstone National Park
1987

GEYSER
Yellowstone National Park
1982

WHAT I ENJOY ABOUT CAMPING
1987

THE HIGH SIERRA FROM GLACIER POINT
Yosemite National Park
1984

The Artists' Camp
1987

DREAMS OF THE MECHANICAL HALF-DOMES
1985

A FLYING PERSON OVER SAN FRANCISCO BAY
1973

SUNRISE 200 FT
1987

LANDSCAPE
Maine 1986

WILDLIFE OF THE PACIFIC NORTHWEST
Oregon 1981

OF COURSE THE SKY IS RED. WHAT DID YOU EXPECT?
USSR 1987

FIREWORKS
Leningrad, USSR 1987

WORLD WAR II VETERAN
Odessa, USSR 1987

Two Young Women
Leningrad, USSR 1987